William Jaroszewski

# RUSSIAN PHRASE BOOK

This phrase book, in a handy pocket size, will help you to be readily understood on all everyday occasions when travelling in Russia; to get you, quickly and easily, *where* you want and *what* you want; and to enable you to cope easily with those minor problems and emergencies that always seem to arise when travelling abroad. Subjects include: customs, travel, sightseeing, eating and drinking, shopping, entertainment, health and leisure activities. An extensive reference section is also included, together with useful background information for the visitor to Russia.

**TEACH YOURSELF BOOKS**

# RUSSIAN
# PHRASE BOOK

TEACH YOURSELF BOOKS
Hodder and Stoughton

*First printed 1961*
*Second edition 1982*

*Copyright © 1961, 1982*
Hodder and Stoughton Ltd

**British Library Cataloguing in Publication Data**

Russian phrase book.—2nd ed.—(Teach
  yourself books)
  1. Russian language—Conversation and
  phrase books
  491.783′421    PG2689

ISBN 0 340 27174 4

*Typeset by Santype International Ltd, Salisbury, Wilts. Printed and bound in Great Britain for Hodder and Stoughton Educational, a division of Hodder and Stoughton Ltd, Mill Road, Dunton Green, Sevenoaks, Kent, by Richard Clay (The Chaucer Press) Ltd, Bungay, Suffolk.*

# Contents

# General Information

Most holidays taken in the USSR are arranged and paid for in advance. Information leaflets are available from *Intourist*, the state tourist information bureau, 292 Regent St, London W1. The tourist is strongly recommended to find out in advance what he wants to see in the town he is visiting. Russians respond warmly to a friendly approach and an interest in their country.

## Opening hours

Business hours vary from place to place but generally shops open early – 8 am–9 am – and close late – 7 pm–9 pm – and close in the middle of the day for one hour.

## Public holidays

Religious festivals are not officially observed in the USSR and their dates do not coincide with those of the Western churches.

The main public holidays are:

| | |
|---|---|
| 1 January | New Year's Day |
| 8 March | International Women's Day |
| 1/2 May | International Labour Day |
| 9 May | Victory Day |
| 7 October | Constitution Day |
| 7/8 November | Anniversary of the Great October Revolution (1917) |

| | |
|---|---|
| The British Embassy | nábirizhnaya Maréesa Taréza, |
| MOSCOW | chitírnatsat. |
| Nab. Maurice Thorez 14 | Británskaye passólstva |

*Medical services* are free in the USSR. Visitors who fall ill should ask the hotel service bureau to call a doctor. In Moscow there is a very well appointed clinic for foreigners: the address is: Gruzínsky piriúlok 3, kórpus 2.

## Tipping

Tipping is practised in the USSR in exactly the same way as in any other country in restaurants, hotels, hairdressers, and to taxi drivers. Chambermaids should be offered about 1 rouble a day; cloakroom attendants 10 kopecks; hairdressers and drivers 10%–15% of the bill or fare. Guides, however, might prefer a recent paperback book to money. This may also apply to other staff – everyone seems to be learning English. Do be careful in your choice of book and avoid anything of a religious, political or pornographic nature. These, as well as similar newspapers and magazines, may be confiscated at the frontier. The best choice is a traditional 'thriller', serious modern novel or a historical novel. Other gifts, instead of books, which are also appreciated include: tights, cosmetics and patterned, polythene carrier bags.

## Emergency telephone numbers

| | |
|---|---|
| Fire | 01 |
| Police | 02 |
| Ambulance | 03 |
| Breakdown service (Moscow) | 04 |

The traditional faith of Russia was the Christian Russian Orthodox Church worship. Several churches in Moscow and other large cities still hold services where the singing and the beauty of the services are very memorable. The hotel or guide will give information. Other forms of worship – Protestant, Catholic, Islam, Judaism – are less common: the Embassy might advise visitors.

## Entering and leaving the USSR

Visitors' luggage is frequently searched and it is not advisable to attempt to 'smuggle' literature or currency, or anything of a controversial nature.

Visitors are forbidden to take any Soviet currency out of the USSR. Foreign currency can only be changed for roubles at official exchange offices, and the receipt for the transaction must be kept and produced on leaving the country. Do *not* accept offers to change currency at a very advantageous rate, made by private individuals. It is a very serious offence to change money illegally, and Russian citizens are not allowed to have foreign currency so, even in discussing such a transaction, the tourist is 'consorting with anti-social elements'.

In the Soviet Union, when walking in the street, people keep to the right.

## Principal tourist attractions

*Moscow*
  The Pushkin Museum of Fine Art
  The Novodévichiy Convent
  The Historical Museum
  The Donskoy Monastery
  The Tretyakov Gallery
  The Andrei Rublev Museum
  The Estates of Ostankino and Arkhangelskoye
  The 'VDNHa' permanent Exhibition
  The Kremlin

*Leningrad*
  The Russian Museum
  The Summer Garden
  The Alexander Nevsky Monastery

The Smolny Cathedral
The Peter and Paul Fortress
Piskaryevskoye Cemetery
Isaac's Cathedral
Kazan Cathedral
Yelagin Palace and Island

Museums are usually open from 10.00 am–8.00 pm. They are open on Sunday, but may be closed on Tuesday. Entrance is inexpensive – usually 10–15 kopecks – and there are lavatories, snack bars and gift shops.

## Other places of interest

Zagorsk (near Moscow); Petrodvorets, Pushkin, Pavlosk (near Leningrad); Vladimir, Suzdal, Pskov, Novgorod, Poltowa.

## Photographs

Do not take photographs of Russians (especially if they are working) without first asking their permission.

*It is forbidden* to photograph: members of the armed forces, bridges, railway stations, frontiers. It is inadvisable to photograph large office blocks or any buildings guarded by a policeman. If in doubt ask 'Mozhna?' (May I?).

## Lavatories

These are usually to be found in streets, parks, cafés and restaurants, but never in shops.

The sign is ТУАЛЕТ (twalyet) and 'men's' – M – (Mushkoy), Ladies – Ж (zhensky).

Public lavatory facilities are free.

## Smoking

There is no smoking in any form of public transport, places of entertainment (theatres, cinemas etc), cafés and shops.

## Litter

Dropping litter, as in most countries, is forbidden.

## Clothing

It cannot be over-emphasised how cold the Russian winter is. Winter visitors to Russia must have a heavy coat, thick hat and gloves or mittens and strong, waterproof boots.

## Some signs and notices

| | |
|---|---|
| Стойте  **Stóyte** | Stop |
| Идите  **Idéetye** | Go |
| Переход  **Pirikhót** | Crossing (or in the Underground, it marks a change to another line) |
| Выход  **Víkhat** | Exit |
| Нет выхода  **Nyét víkhada** | No exit |
| Вход  **Fkhót** | Entrance |
| Нет входа  **Nyét fkhóda** | No entrance |
| В город  **V górat** | To the town |
| Держитесь левой (правой) стороны  **Dirzhéetyes lyévay (právay) staranée** | Keep to the left (right) |
| Метро  **Mitróh** | Underground |
| К поездам  **K payezdám** | To the trains |
| Берегитесь!  **Birigéetyes** | Look out! Warning! |
| Осторóжно, здесь ступéнька  **Astarózhna, zdyés stupyénka** | Mind the step |
| Опáсно  **Apássna** | Danger |

| | |
|---|---|
| Вход запрещён **Fkhód zaprishchón** | No admittance |
| Про́сят не ходи́ть по траве́ **Prósyat ni khadéet pa travyéh** | Please keep off the grass |
| Остерега́йтесь соба́ки! **Astirigáytyes sabáky** | Beware of the dog |
| Остерега́йтесь воро́в! **Astirigáytyes varóf** | Beware of pickpockets |
| Отсю́да мо́жно телефони́ровать **Atsyúda mózhna tilifaníravat** | You may telephone from here |
| Запасно́й вы́ход **Zapasnóy víkhat** | Emergency exit |
| Толка́ть от себя́ **(Talkát) at sibyáh** | Push |
| Тяну́ть к себе́ **(Tyinút) k sibyéh** | Pull |
| Почи́нка доро́ги **Pachéenka darógy** | Road repairs; road up |
| Ме́дленный ход **Myédlinny khot** | Go slow |
| Объе́зд **Abyézd** | Diversion |
| Нет прое́зда **Nyét prayézda** | No through way; no thoroughfare |
| Движе́ние то́лько в одно́м направле́нии **Dvizhénye tólka v adnóm napravlyéniy** | One-way street |
| Впереди́ гла́вная у́лица (доро́га) **Fpiridée glávnaya úlitsa (daróga)** | Main road ahead |
| Кури́ть запреща́ется **Kuréet zaprishcháyitsya** | No smoking |
| Куре́ние стро́го заприщено́ **Kuryénye stróga zaprishchinóh** | Smoking strictly forbidden |

# Alphabet and Pronunciation

## The Russian alphabet

| Cap | Small | Rough | English equivalent |
|-----|-------|-------|--------------------|
| А | а | a | as in father |
| Б | б | b | as in bun |
| В | в | v | as in vine |
| Г | г | g | as in gun |
| Д | д | d | as in dog |
| Е | е | ye | as in yet |
| Ё | ё | yo | as in yonder |
| Ж | ж | s | as in pleasure |
| З | з | z | as in zebra |
| И | и | ee | as in meet |
| Й | й | y | as in boy |
| К | к | k | as in king |
| Л | л | l | usually as in Cockney 'battle' |
| М | м | m | as in mat |
| Н | н | n | as in not |
| О | о | o | as in north |
| П | п | p | as in pot |
| Р | р | r | as in rat |
| С | с | s | as in sand |
| Т | т | t | as in tank (but with a touch of 'th') |
| У | у | oo | as in book (as a northerner would say it) |
| Ф | ф | f | as in fig |
| Х | х | h | as in heaven (*not* as guttural as lo*ch*) |
| Ц | ц | ts | as in hits |
| Ч | ч | ch | as in cheque |
| Ш | ш | sh | as in short |
| Щ | щ | shch | as in push-chair |
| | ъ | – | Hard sign; not pronounced |
| | ы | i | as in Cockney 'Bill' |

| Cap | Small | Rough | English equivalent |
|-----|-------|-------|--------------------|
|     | ь     | –     | soft sign; softens preceding consonant with slight y sound, as in canyon |
| Э   | э     | e     | as in met |
| Ю   | ю     | you   | as in you, but slightly shorter |
| Я   | я     | ya    | as in yard |

## Pronunciation

The transcription given is a rough guide to the sound of spoken Russian. The visitor who knows no Russian should be able to make himself understood if he reads the transcribed words exactly as if he were speaking English.

The only points to note are:

ee is pronounced as in 'see'.
zh is pronounced like the 's' in measure.
u is pronounced as a long 'oo' as in 'fool'.

The *stressed* syllables should be pronounced *very clearly*.

However, the visitor should try to master the alphabet, if only in order to find his way about.

## Note on stress

The stress in Russian is most important. It is very strongly emphasised. The stressed vowel is very clearly marked in this book. It should be pronounced in what appears to English ears a very exaggerated way. Always over-emphasise the stressed syllable.

*Unstressed vowels*

Having located the stressed vowel in each word, any other vowels in the word should be pronounced more quickly, and without their full value. We do the same in English. Listen to yourself saying the word 'immediately', and you will understand what the Russians do. The vowel 'a' becomes a mere 'uh' noise, as in 'but'.

As a rough guide, the vowels in the unstressed position are pronounced as follows:

a and o have an indeterminate value like the 'u' in the English word 'but'.

e and я are pronounced like the 'i' in the English word 'hit', except at the beginning of words, when the sound is 'yi', as in 'Yiddish'.

This is by far the most important thing about Russian pronunciation. It is beyond the limits of this work to give a more detailed account of the phonetics of Russian. Those who wish to pursue the subject are recommended to study a grammar book which has a phonetic section.

N.B. The vowel ё is *always* stressed. When a word contains this vowel you will see no stress marked. This vowel does not count as a separate letter of the Russian alphabet, and not all books print the two dots over it, but print simply e. However, all elementary books now print it as ё.

# Everyday Words and Phrases

## Language problems

Are you a foreigner?
**Vi inastránits?**
Вы иностра́нец?

I am an Englishman (woman)
**Ya anglichánin (anglichánka)**
Я англича́нин (англича́нка)

I am an American
**Ya amirikánits (amirikánka)**
Я америка́нец (америка́нка)

Can I visit the Soviet Union?
**Magú ya pasitéet Saviétsky Sayúz?**
Могу́ я посети́ть Сове́тский Сою́з?

I am French by birth
**Ya frantsús pa praeeskhazhdyényu**
Я францу́з по происхожде́нию

I am German by marriage
**Ya nyémka pa múzhu**
Я не́мка по́ мужу

Do you speak English (French, German)?
**Vi gavaréetye p-angléesky (pa-frantsúsky, pa-nimyétsky)?**
Вы говори́те по-англи́йски (по-францу́зски, по-неме́цки)?

I speak only a little English
**Ya gavaryú tólka nimnóga p-angléesky**
Я говорю́ то́лько немно́го по-англи́йски

I can read a little, but not talk
**Ya nimnóga chitáyu, no ni gavaryú**
Я немно́го чита́ю, но не говорю́

Can you understand me?
**Vi minyá panimáyitye?**
Вы меня́ понима́ете?

Please speak a little slower

**Pazhálusta, gavaréetye nimnóga myédlinyeye**

Пожáлуйста, говорúте немнóго мéдленнее

I didn't understand you

**Ya vass ni pónyal**

Я вас не пóнял

Could you translate this for me?

**Ni mózhitye ly vi pirivesteé mnyé éta?**

Не мóжете ли вы перевестú мне э́то?

Russian seems to me a very difficult language

**Mnyé rússky yazík kázhitsya óchin trúdnim**

Мне рýсский язы́к кáжется óчень трýдным

I need an interpreter

**Mnyé núzhin pirivódchik**

Мне нýжен перевóдчик

## Enquiries

What is your first name?

**Kak váshe éemya?**

Как вáше úмя?

What is your surname?

**Kak vásha faméelya?**

Как вáша фамúлия?

Where do you live?

**Gdyé vi zhivyótye?**

Где вы живёте?

What is your address?

**Kakóy vash ádriss?**

Какóй ваш áдрес?

What is your telephone number?

**Kakóy nómir váshiva tilifóna?**

Какóй нóмер вáшего телефóна?

What do you do?

**Kto vi?**

Кто вы?

Do you speak English?

**Vi gavaréetye p-angléesky?**

Вы говорúте по-англúйски?

Do you understand me?

**Vi panimáyitye minyá?**

Вы понимáете меня́?

Who is that?

**Kto éta takóy?**

Кто э́то такóй?

| | |
|---|---|
| What is that? (What is this?) | **Shto éta takóye?** |
| | Что э́то тако́е? |
| What is that called? | **Kak éta naziváyitsya?** |
| | Как э́то называ́ется? |
| What is that for? | **Dlyá chivóh éta?** |
| | Для чего́ э́то? |
| Which? | **Katóry?** |
| | Кото́рый? |
| What (kind of)? | **Kakóy?** |
| | Како́й? |
| Where? | **Gdyé?** |
| | Где? |
| Where to? | **Kudá?** |
| | Куда́? |
| From where? | **Atkúda?** |
| | Отку́да? |
| When? | **Kagdá?** |
| | Когда́? |
| How long? | **Skólka vryéminy?** |
| | Ско́лько вре́мени? |
| What price? | **Kakáya tsináh?** |
| | Кака́я цена́? |
| How much does this cost? | **Skólka éta stóyit?** |
| | Ско́лько э́то сто́ит? |
| How much do I owe you? | **Skólka yá vam dólzhin?** |
| | Ско́лько я вам до́лжен? |
| Why? (=What is the reason?) | **Pachimú?** |
| | Почему́? |
| Why? (=For what purpose?) | **Zachém?** |
| | Заче́м? |
| How far from here (from there)? | **Kak dalikóh atsyúda (attúda)?** |
| | Как далеко́ отсю́да (отту́да)? |
| How can one get there? | **Kak tudá praytee (prayékhat)?** |
| | Как туда́ пройти́ (прое́хать)? |
| Is there a telephone here? | **Yést zdyés tilifón?** |
| | Есть здесь телефо́н? |
| Have you time now? | **Yést u vass vryémya tipyér?** |
| | Есть у вас вре́мя тепе́рь? |

| | |
|---|---|
| Can you tell me? | **Mózhitye vi skazát mnyé?**<br>Мо́жете вы сказа́ть мне? |
| Can one (I) get tickets? | **Mózhna (magú yá) dastát bilyéty?**<br>Мо́жно (могу́ я) доста́ть биле́ты? |
| May I come in? | **Mózhna vaytée?**<br>Мо́жно войти́? |
| Is it possible to go in now? | **Uzhéh mózhna vkhadéet?**<br>Уже́ мо́жно входи́ть? |
| Is it not possible to get in yet? | **Yishchóh nilzyá vkhadéet?**<br>Ещё нельзя́ входи́ть? |
| Do I have to get permission?<br>Must (should) I get permission? | **Dólzhin yá (náda) paluchéet razrishénye?**<br>До́лжен я (на́до) получи́ть разреше́ние? |
| What do you want (wish)? | **Shto vi khatéetye?**<br>Что вы хоти́те?<br>**Shto vam ugódna?**<br>Что вам уго́дно? |
| What do you want (need)? | **Shto vam núzhna?**<br>Что вам ну́жно? |
| Where are you going? | **Kudá vi idyótye (yédyetye)?**<br>Куда́ вы идёте (е́дете)? |
| When are you leaving? | **Kagdá vi uyezháyitye?**<br>Когда́ вы уезжа́ете? |
| When will you come? | **Kagdá vi pridyótye (priyédyetye)?**<br>Когда́ вы придёте (прие́дете)? |
| When will you be at home? | **Kagdá vi búditye dóma?**<br>Когда́ вы бу́дете до́ма? |
| What do you think about that? | **Shto vi dúmayitye ab étam?**<br>Что вы ду́маете об э́том? |
| What is your opinion? | **Kakóye váshe mnyénye?**<br>Како́е ва́ше мне́ние? |
| Do you know about this? | **Znáyitye vi ab étam?**<br>Зна́ете вы об э́том? |
| Can you give me some information? | **Mózhitye vi dat mnyé svyédinya?**<br>Мо́жете вы дать мне све́дения? |

## Paying a visit

| | |
|---|---|
| Did you ring? | **Vi zvaneély?** |
| | Вы звони́ли? |
| Is ... at home? | **... dóma?** |
| | ... до́ма? |
| Please come in | **Vaydeétye, pazhálusta** |
| | Войди́те, пожа́луйста |
| ... wishes to speak to you | **... zhiláyit s vámy pagavareét** |
| | ... жела́ет с ва́ми поговори́ть |
| I'm very pleased to see you | **Óchin rat (ráda) vass veédyet** |
| | О́чень рад (ра́да) вас ви́деть |
| You are very welcome! | **Meélosty prósim!** |
| | Ми́лости про́сим! |
| This is a great pleasure for me (us) | **Éta balshóye udavólstvye dlyá minyá (dlyá nass)** |
| | Э́то большо́е удово́льствие для меня́ (для нас) |
| It was very kind of you to invite me | **Bwíla óchin lyubyézna s váshey staraníy minyá priglasseét** |
| | Бы́ло о́чень любе́зно с ва́шей стороны́ меня́ пригласи́ть |
| You are very kind | **Vi óchin lyubyézny** |
| | Вы о́чень любе́зны |
| I'm late (early) | **Ya apazdál (priyékhal rána)** |
| | Я опозда́л (прие́хал ра́но) |
| Allow me to introduce my husband to you | **Razrisheétye pridstávit vam mayivóh múzha** |
| | Разреши́те предста́вить вам моего́ му́жа |
| How do you do? | **Óchin preeátna paznakómitsya?** |
| | О́чень прия́тно познако́миться? |
| Here are my son and daughter | **Vot móy siýn ee mayáh doch** |
| | Вот мой сын и моя́ дочь |
| Please sit down | **Sadeétyes, pazhálusta** |
| | Сади́тесь, пожа́луйста |
| May I offer you tea? | **Mózhna pridlazheét vam cháyu?** |
| | Мо́жно предложи́ть вам ча́ю? |

| | |
|---|---|
| Stay and have some tea (dinner, supper) with us (me) | **Astántyes vípeet cháyu (pa-abyédat, paúzhinat) s námy (sa mnóy)** |
| | Останьтесь выпить чаю (пообедать, поужинать) с нами (со мной) |
| I'm sorry, but I must go | **K sazhalyényu, yá ni magú astátsya dólshe** |
| | К сожалению, я должен идти (уходить) |
| I do hope you'll come again soon | **Nadyéyuss, shto vi skóra apyát pridyótye (priyédyetye)** |
| | Надеюсь, что вы скоро опять придёте (приедете) |
| Come whenever you like | **Prikhadéetye (priyezháytye) v lyubóye vryémya** |
| | Приходите (приезжайте) в любое время |
| You are always welcome | **Vi vsyigdá zhilánny gost (zhilánnaya góstya)** |
| | Вы всегда желанный гость (желанная гостья) |
| Thank you very much for your kind welcome (hospitality) | **Balshóye spasséeba za radúshny priyóm (gastipriyéemstva)** |
| | Большое спасибо за радушный приём (гостеприймство) |
| Remember me to your parents | **Klanyáytyes váshim radéetyilyam** |
| | Кланяйтесь вашим родителям |
| Give them my regards | **Piridáytye yéem privyét** |
| | Передайте им привет |

## Small talk

| | | |
|---|---|---|
| How do you do? Hullo! | **Zdrástvuytye** | Здравствуйте! |
| Good afternoon | **Dóbry dyén** | Добрый день |
| Good evening | **Dóbry vyéchir** | Добрый вечер |
| (Used only when meeting *not* parting) | | |

| Good morning | **Dóbraye útra** | Доброе утро |
| Good night | **Spakóyny nóchy** | Спокойной ночи |
| (Used only when getting up and going to bed) | | |
| How are things? | **Kak vi pazhiváyitye?** | Как вы поживаете? |
| All right. And with you? | **Kharashóh. A vi?** | Хорошо. А вы? |
| Yes, all right too | **Yá tózhe kharashóh** | Я тоже хорошо |
| Fair. So-so | **Tak sibyéh** | Так себе |
| Pleased to see you | **Rat (ráda, rády) vass véedyet** | Рад (рада, рады) вас видеть |
| Haven't seen you for a long time | **Davnóh vass ni véedyel(a)** | Давно вас не видел(а) |
| How very pleasant! | **Óchin preeátna!** | Очень приятно! |
| Au revoir | **Da svidánya** | До свидания! |
| See you again soon | **Da skórava svidánya** | До скорого свидания |
| All the best | **Vsyevóh kharóshiva!** (**Vsyevóh lúch- shiva, vsyevóh dóbrava!**) | Всего хорошего! (Всего лучшего! Всего доброго!) |
| Keep well | **Búdtye zdaróvy!** | Будьте здоровы! |
| Have a pleasant trip! (Short) | **Preeátnava putée!** | Приятного пути! |
| Don't forget us | **Ni zabiváytye nass!** | Не забывайте нас |
| Good-bye; farewell | **Prashcháytye!** | Прощайте! |
| Congratulations! | **Pazdravlyáyu vass!** | Поздравляю вас! |
| Happy New Year! | **(Pazdravlyáyu) s Nóvim Gódam!** | (Поздравляю) с Новым годом! |
| Many Happy Returns! | **(Pazdravlyáyu) sa dnyóm razhdyé- nya!** | (Поздравляю) со днём рождения! |
| Happy holiday! (One-day type) | **(Pazdravlyáyu) c práznikam!** | (Поздравляю) с праздником! |
| I (we) wish you health (happiness, success) | **Zhiláyu (zhiláyim) vam zdaróvya (shchástya, uspyékha)** | Желаю (желаем) вам здоровья (счастья, успеха) |

| | | |
|---|---|---|
| Pleasant journey | **(Zhiláyu vam) shchastleévava puteé!** | (Желáю вам) счастлúвого путú! |
| Glad you've arrived | **C priyézdam!** | С приéздом! |
| Wishes | **Pazhilánya** | Пожелáния |

## Requests

| | | |
|---|---|---|
| Please . . . | **Pazhálusta** | Пожáлуйста |
| Be so good (kind) as to . . . | **Búdtye dabríy (lyubyézny)** | Бýдьте добры́ (любéзны) |
| I request you, ask you, to . . . | **Prashú vass** | Прошý вас |
| Give | **Dáytye** | Дáйте |
| Bring | **Prinesseétye** | Принесúте |
| Take away | **Unisseétye** | Унесúте |
| Put (in a lying position) | **Palazhéetye** | Положúте |
| Put (in a standing position) | **Pastáftye** | Постáвьте |
| Hang (something) up | **Pavyéstye** | Повéсьте |
| Open (shut) | **Atkróytye (zakróytye)** | Открóйте (закрóйте) |
| Help | **Pamageétye** | Помогúте |
| Do | **Sdyélaytye** | Сдéлайте |
| Read | **Prachteétye** | Прочтúте |
| Write | **Napisheétye** | Напишúте |
| Translate | **Pirivideétye** | Переведúте |
| Explain | **Abyasneétye** | Объяснúте |
| Tell (say) | **Skazhéetye** | Скажúте |
| Show | **Pakazhéetye** | Покажúте |
| Take (somebody) to . . . | **Pravadeétye** | Проводúте |
| Buy | **Kupéetye** | Купúте |
| Lend | **Adalzhéetye** | Одолжúте |

|  |  |  |
|---------|-----------------|---------|
| Listen | **Paslúshaytye** | Послýшайте |
| Look | **Pasmatréetye** | Посмотрúте |
| Come here | **Padéetye syudá** | Подúте сюдá |
| Follow me! | **Idéetye (payezháy-tye) za mnóy** | Идúте (поез-жáйте) за мной |
| Go (drive) ahead (back) | **Idéetye (payezháy-tye) fpiryót (nazát)** | Идúте (поез-жáйте) вперёд (назáд) |
| Move on! (Drive on!) | **Prakhadéetye (prayezháytye)!** | Проходúте (проезжáйте)! |
| Do not stop! | **Ni astanávlivay-tyes!** | Не останáвли-вайтесь! |
| Call a taxi | **Pazavéetye taksée!** | Позовúте таксú |
| Start | **Payezháytye!** | Поезжáйте! |
| Stop! Halt! Stand still! | **Stóytye!** | Стóйте! |
| Stop (doing something, e.g. making a noise) | **Piristántye (shumyét)** | Перестáньте (шумéть) |

| | |
|---|---|
| Please give me a cup of coffee | **Pazhálusta, dáytye cháshku kófye** |
| | Пожáлуйста, дáйте чáшку кóфе |
| Give me a match, please | **Dáytye spéechku, pazhálusta** |
| | Дáйте спúчку, пожáлуйста |
| Be so good (kind) as to post this letter | **Búdtye tak dabríy (lyubyézny), apustéetye éta peessmóh** |
| | Бýдьте так добры́ (любéзны), опустúте э́то письмó |
| Do me a favour | **Sdyélaytye mnyé adalzhénya** |
| | Сдéлайте мне одолжéние |
| I have a request to make | **U minyá k vam prózba** |
| | У меня́ к вам прóсьба |
| Could you help me? | **Ni mózhitye ly vi mnyé pamóch?** |
| | Не мóжете ли вы мне помóчь? |
| I don't want to be disturbed | **Prashú minyá ni bispakóyit** |
| | Прошý меня́ не беспокóить |

## Asking permission

Is smoking allowed?

**Mózhna zdyés kuréet?**
Мóжно здесь курúть?

May I (we) come in?

**Magú yá (mózhim mi) vaytée?**
Могý я (мóжем мы) войтú?

May I have your permission to smoke (borrow your paper)?

**Razrishéetye (pazvóltye) kuréet (vzyát váshu gazyétu)**
Разрешúте (позвóльте) курúть (взять вáшу газéту)

## Refusing permission

Smoking is forbidden here

**Zdyés nilzyá kuréet**
Здесь нельзя́ курúть

You can't go in at the moment

**Sicháss nilzyá vkhadéet**
Сейчáс нельзя́ входúть

## Offering help

Shall I open the window?

**Atkrít aknóh**
Открúть окнó?

May I help you?

**Pamóch vam?**
Помóчь вам?

Can I give you some money?

**Dat vam dyényig?**
Дать вам дéнег?

Would you like a cigarette (to look at my paper)?

**Khatéetye papiróssu (pasmatryét móy zhurnál)?**
Хотúте папирóсу (посмотрéть мой журнáл)?

Yes, please!

**Pazhálusta!**
Пожáлуйста!

## Invitation

Would you like to come to the pictures?

**Ni khatéetye ly paytée f keenóh?**
Не хотúте ли пойтú в кинó?

Do you want to go to the pictures?

**Khatéetye paytée f keenóh?**
Хотúте пойтú в кинó?

| | |
|---|---|
| Let's go to the pictures | **Paydyómtye f keenóh**<br>Пойдёмте в кино́ |
| Let's go to Leningrad | **Payédyemtye v Liningrát**<br>Пое́демте в Ленингра́д |
| Come to the pictures with us! | **Paydyómtye s námy f keenóh**<br>Пойдёмте с на́ми в кино́ |
| Come and have dinner with us tomorrow | **Prikhadéetye k nam záftra abyédat**<br>Приходи́те к нам за́втра обе́дать |
| Come and stay with us | **Astanavéetyes u nass**<br>Останови́тесь у нас |
| Do please come in | **Fkhadéetye, pazhálusta**<br>Входи́те, пожа́луйста |
| Thank you, with pleasure | **Spasséeba, s udavólstvyem**<br>Спаси́бо, с удово́льствием |
| I'm sorry I can't (we can't) | **K sazhalyényu, ni magú (mi ni mózhim)**<br>К сожале́нию, не могу́ (мы не мо́жем) |
| Without fail (I shall come) | **Niprimyénna (pridú)**<br>Непреме́нно (приду́) |

## Agreement, disagreement

| | | |
|---|---|---|
| Wonderful!<br>  Marvellous! | **Vilikalyépna!**<br>  **Prikrásna!** | Великоле́пно!<br>  Прекра́сно! |
| Good! | **Kharashóh!** | Хорошо́! |
| I agree | **Yá saglássyin (saglássna)** | Я согла́сен (согла́сна) |
| We agree | **Mi saglássny** | Мы согла́сны |
| I disagree | **Yá ni saglássyin** | Я не согла́сен |
| I refuse | **Ya atkázivayus** | Я отка́зываюсь |
| I agree (disagree) with you | **Yá s vámy saglássyin (nisaglássyin)** | Я с вами согла́сен (несогла́сен) |
| You are right (wrong) | **Vi právy (niprávy)** | Вы пра́вы (непра́вы) |

| | | |
|---|---|---|
| You are mistaken | **Vi ashibáyityes** | Вы ошибáетесь |
| You have no right | **Vi ni imyéyitye prava** | Вы не имéете прáва |
| You cannot compel me (make me) | **Vi ni mózhitye zastávit minyá** | Вы не мóжете застáвить меня |

## Liking, satisfaction, wish, need

| | | |
|---|---|---|
| I (very much) like this city (these drawings) | **Mnyé (óchin)** { | **nrávitsya état górat** <br> **nrávyatsya éty rissúnky** |
| | **Мне (óчень)** { | нрáвится этот гóрод <br> нрáвятся эти рисýнки |
| I (very much) liked the concert (play, performance, paintings) | **Mnyé (óchin)** { | **panrávilsya kantsért** <br> **panrávilas pyéssa** <br> **panrávilas pridstavlyénye** <br> **panrávilis kartéeny** |
| | **Мне (óчень)** { | понрáвился концéрт <br> понрáвилась пьéса <br> понрáвилось представлéние <br> понрáвились картины |
| You will like . . . | **Vam panrávitsya (panrávyatsya)** . . . | |
| | Вам понрáвится (понрáвятся) . . . | |
| I (very much) like (we like), I am (we are) very fond of music | **Yá (óchin) lyublyú (mi lyúbim) múziku** | |
| | Я (óчень) люблю (мы любим) мýзыку | |

| | |
|---|---|
| I am (we are) pleased with the house, the work, everything | **Yá davólyin (davólna, mi davólny) dómam, rabótay, vsyóm**<br>Я дово́лен (дово́льна, мы дово́льны) до́мом, рабо́той, всём |
| I (we) should like to go to India | **Yá khatyél(a) bi (mi khatyély bi) payékhat f Eéndiyu**<br>Я хоте́л(а) бы (мы хоте́ли бы) пое́хать в И́ндию |
| I (we) want | **Yá khachú (mi khatéem)**<br>Я хочу́ (мы хоти́м) |
| I (we) feel like a sleep (a smoke, something to eat) | **Mnyé (nam) khóchitsya spat (pakuréet, yést)**<br>Мне (нам) хо́чется спать (покури́ть, есть) |
| I need a permit | **Mnyé núzhin própusk**<br>Мне ну́жен про́пуск |
| I need help | **Mnyé nuzhnáh pómashch**<br>Мне нужна́ по́мощь |
| I need permission | **Mnyé nuzhnóh razrishénye**<br>Мне нужно́ разреше́ние |
| I need money | **Mnyé nuzhneé dyéngy**<br>Мне нужны́ де́ньги |
| He needed a permit | **Yimú núzhin bwil própusk**<br>Ему́ ну́жен был про́пуск |
| He needed help | **Yimú nuzhnáh bwiláh pómashch**<br>Ему́ нужна́ была́ по́мощь |
| He needed permission | **Yimú nuzhnóh bwila razrishénye**<br>Ему́ нужно́ бы́ло разреше́ние |
| He needed money | **Yimú nuzhneé bwíly dyéngy**<br>Ему́ нужны́ бы́ли де́ньги |
| You will need a permit | **Vam núzhin búdyit própusk**<br>Вам ну́жен бу́дет про́пуск |
| You will need help | **Vam nuzhnáh búdyit pómashch**<br>Вам нужна́ бу́дет по́мощь |
| You will need permission | **Vam nuzhnóh búdyit razrishénye**<br>Вам нужно́ бу́дет разреше́ние |

## Miscellaneous expressions

| | | |
|---|---|---|
| Of course, certainly | **Kanyéshna** | Конéчно |
| No doubt, undoubtedly | **Nisamnyénna** | Несомнéнно |
| I am sure | **Yá uvyérin(a)** | Я увéрен(a) |
| Probably | **Virayátna** | Вероя́тно |
| Perhaps, may be | **Mózhit bwit** | Мóжет быть |
| I think (=I am not *sure*) | **Kázhitsya** | Кáжется |
| Indeed? | **F sámam dyélye** | В сáмом дéле? |

## Expressions of thanks

| | |
|---|---|
| Thank you | **Blagadaryú vass** |
| | Благодарю́ вас |
| Thank you very much | **Blagadaryú vass óchin** |
| | Благодарю́ вас óчень |
| Thanks | **Spasséeba** |
| | Спасúбо |
| Thanks very much | **Balsháya spasséeba** |
| | Большóе спасúбо |
| Thank you for the present | **Blagadaryú vass za padárak** |
| | Благодарю́ вас за подáрок |
| Not at all | **Ni stóyit** |
| | Не стóит |
| Not at all | **Nyéh za shto** |
| | Нé за что |
| You are very kind | **Vi óchin dabríy** |
| | Вы óчень добры́ |
| I am very grateful to you | **Yá vam óchin blagadáryin (blagadárna)** |
| | Я вам óчень благодáрен (благодáрна) |
| I am very much obliged to you | **Yá vam óchin abyázan** |
| | Я вам óчень обя́зан |

| | |
|---|---|
| I'm deeply indebted to you | **Yá v balshóm dalgú pyérid vámy**<br>Я в большо́м долгу́ пе́ред ва́ми |
| You have done me a great favour | **Vi mnyé sdyélaly balshóye adalzhénye**<br>Вы мне сде́лали большо́е одолже́ние |
| I wish I were in a position to repay you | **Yá khatyél bi bwít f sástayániy vam atplatéet**<br>Я хоте́л бы быть в состоя́нии вам отплати́ть |
| Please accept my sincere thanks | **Priméetye moyú éeskrinnyuyu blagadárnast**<br>Прими́те мою́ и́скреннюю благода́рность |

# Expressions of apology and regret

| | |
|---|---|
| I beg your pardon | **Prastéetye**<br>Прости́те |
| Excuse me (I'm sorry) | **Izvinéetye (izvinyáyus)**<br>Извини́те (извиня́юсь) |
| Sorry! My fault! | **Vinavát**<br>Винова́т! |
| Not at all! Don't worry | **Nichivóh! Ni bispakóytyes**<br>Ничего́! Не беспоко́йтесь |
| I'm sorry I'm late | **Izvinéetye, shto ya apazdál(a)**<br>Извини́те, что я опозда́л(а) |
| It's my fault; I'm wrong | **Yá vinavát(a)**<br>Я винова́т(а) |
| It wasn't my fault | **Éta bwíla ni pa mayéy vinyéh**<br>Это бы́ло не по мое́й вине́ |
| I didn't do it on purpose | **Yá éta sdyélala ni naróshna**<br>Я э́то сде́лал(а) не наро́чно |
| Don't be angry | **Ni sirdéetyes**<br>Не серди́тесь |
| Don't be offended | **Ni abizháytyes**<br>Не обижа́йтесь |

Don't think me impolite (rude)

**Ni schitáytye minyá nivyézhlivim (grúbim)**
Не считáйте меня невéжливым (грýбым)

I regret the misunderstanding

**Ya sazhalyéyu a nidarazumyéniy**
Я сожалéю о недоразумéнии

It's a pity

**Óchin zhal**
Óчень жаль

I am sorry for you

**Mnyé vass zhal**
Мне вас жаль

# On Arrival

## Issue and inspection of documents

| | | |
|---|---|---|
| Passport | **Pásspart** | Па́спорт |
| Identification papers | **Udastaviryénye léechnasty** | Удостовере́ние ли́чности |
| Visa (entry, exit) | **Véeza (na vyézd, na víyezd)** | Ви́за (на въезд, на вы́езд) |
| Permission to stay for a period (for a break of journey) | **Razrishénye na pribiványe (na astanófku f putée)** | Разреше́ние на пребыва́ние (на остано́вку в пути́) |
| Purpose of journey | **Tséyl payézdky** | Цель пое́здки |
| Surname | **Faméeliya** | Фами́лия |
| First name | **Eémya** | И́мя |
| Nationality | **Natsyanálnast (pódanstva)** | Национа́льность (по́дданство) |
| Signature | **Pódpiss** | По́дпись |

What is your surname?

**Kak vásha faméeliya?**
Как ва́ша фами́лия?

What is your first name?

**Kak váshe éemya?**
Как ва́ше и́мя?

What is your nationality?

**Kakáya vásha natsyanálnast?**
Кака́я ва́ша национа́льность?

I am an Englishman (woman)

**Ya anglichánin (anglichánka)**
Я англича́нин (англича́нка)

I am a British subject

**Ya angléesky pódanny (Ya angléeskaya pódanaya)**
Я англи́йский по́дданный (англи́йская по́дданная)

Show your passport

**Pridyavéetye vash pásspart**
Покажи́те (предъяви́те) ваш па́спорт

| | | |
|---|---|---|
| What is the object of your journey (arrival) to the USSR? | **Kakáya tséyl váshy payézdky (váshiva priyézda) f SSSR?** | |
| | Кака́я цель ва́шей пое́здки (ва́шего прие́зда) в СССР? | |
| I am a tourist | **Ya turéest** | |
| | Я тури́ст | |
| I am a member of a delegation | **Ya chlyén diligátsy** | |
| | Я член делега́ции | |
| I belong to a party (of students) | **Ya chlyén grúppy (studyéntaf)** | |
| | Я член гру́ппы (студе́нтов) | |
| Have you been to the USSR before? | **Bwíly vi ránshe f SSSR?** | |
| | Бы́ли вы ра́ньше в СССР? | |
| Yes, last year | **Da, f próshlam gadú** | |
| | Да, в про́шлом году́ | |
| No, I am here for the first time | **Nyét, ya zdyés f pyérvy rass** | |
| | Нет, я здесь в пе́рвый раз | |
| Can I extend my visa? | **Magú ya pradléet véezu?** | |
| | Могу́ я продли́ть ви́зу? | |
| Help me to fill in this form | **Pamagéetye mnyé zapólnit état blank (étu ankyétu)** | |
| | Помоги́те мне запо́лнить э́тот бланк (э́ту анке́ту) | |
| Where do I have to sign? | **Gdyé padpissátsya?** | |
| | Где подписа́ться? | |
| How much do I have to pay? | **Skólka platéet?** | |
| | Ско́лько плати́ть? | |
| When will you return my passport? | **Kagdá vi virnyótye mnyé pásspart?** | |
| | Когда́ вы верне́те мне па́спорт? | |
| Where is the British consulate? | **Gdyé británskaye kónsulstva?** | |
| | Где брита́нское ко́нсульство? | |

## Customs examination

| | | |
|---|---|---|
| Customs house | **Tamózhnya** | Тамо́жня |
| Duty | **Póshlina** | По́шлина |
| Luggage | **Bagásh** | Бага́ж |

| Tobacco | **Tabák** | Табáк |
| Cigars | **Sigáry** | Сигáры |
| Perfume | **Dukhée** | Духи́ |
| Camera | **Fata-aparát** | Фотоаппарáт |
| Articles liable to duty | **Vyéshchy padlizhá-shchy póshlinye (aplátye)** | Вéщи подлежá-щие пóшлине (оплáте) |
| Foreign currency | **Valyúta** | Валю́та |

| | | |
|---|---|---|
| Where will the luggage be examined? | **Gdyé búdut asmátrivat bagásh?** | |
| | Где бýдут осмáтривать багáж? | |
| Where is the customs? | **Gdyé tamózhnya?** | |
| | Где тамóжня? | |
| Take my luggage to the customs | **Sniséetye moy bagásh f tamózhnyu** | |
| | Снеси́те мой багáж в тамóжню | |
| Have you anything to declare? | **Yést u vass shtó-nibut shto padlizhéet aplátye?** | |
| | Есть у вас чтó-нибудь, что подлежи́т оплáте? | |
| Shall I open this case? | **Atkrít état chimadán?** | |
| | Откры́ть э́тот чемодáн? | |
| I have nothing to declare | **U minyá nichivó nyét zayivéet** | |
| | У меня́ ничегó нет заяви́ть | |
| I have only things for personal use | **U minyá tólka vyéshchy dlyá léechnava pólzavanya** | |
| | У меня́ тóлько вéщи для ли́чного пóльзования | |
| Have you any of the articles on the list? | **Yést u vass shtó-nibut eez pridmyétaf na spéeskye?** | |
| | Есть у вас чтó-нибудь из предмéтов на спи́ске? | |
| Have you any spirits or tobacco? | **Yést u vass spéert éely tabák?** | |
| | Есть у вас спирт или табáк? | |
| I have only a small bottle of perfume | **U minyá tólka nibalshóy flakón dukhóf** | |
| | У меня́ тóлько небольшóй флакóн духóв | |

This is dutiable

**Éta padlizhéet aplátye**

Это подлежи́т опла́те

You have to pay duty on this

**Za éta vi dalzhnée platéet póshlinu**

За э́то вы должны́ плати́ть по́шлину

How much is the duty?

**Skólka platéet póshlinu?**

Ско́лько плати́ть по́шлины?

Is my luggage passed?

**Prapúshchin móy bagásh?**

Пропу́щен мой бага́ж?

Is that all?

**Éta vsyóh?**

Это всё?

I shall retain this

**Ya zadirzhú éta**

Я задержу́ э́то

We shall return this to you when you leave the USSR

**Mi virnyóm vam éta prée víyezde eez SSSR**

Мы вернём вам э́то при вы́езде из СССР

Here is your receipt

**Vot vam rasspéeska**

Вот вам распи́ска

You must declare how much foreign currency you have

**Vi dalzhnée zayivéet skólka u vass valyúty**

Вы должны́ заяви́ть, ско́лько у вас валю́ты

Fill in this form

**Zapólneetye état blank**

Заполни́те э́тот бланк

Bear in mind that it is forbidden to export Soviet currency

**Imyétye v veedú shto sovyétskiye dyéngy vivazéet nilzyá**

Име́йте в виду́, что сове́тские де́ньги вывози́ть нельзя́

You must spend it all in the Soviet Union

**Vi dalzhnée istrátit eekh vsyéh f Savyétskam Sayúze**

Вы должны́ истра́тить их все в Сове́тском Сою́зе

## Money exchange

| | | |
|---|---|---|
| Money | **Dyéngy** | Дéньги |
| Rate of exchange | **Kúrss** | Курс |
| Official | **Afitsyálny** | Официáльный |
| Tourist | **Turéestsky** | Турúстский |
| Traveller's cheque | **Turéestsky chek** | Турúстский чек |
| Note | **Bilyét** | Билéт |
| Large | **Krúpny** | Крýпный |
| Small | **Myélky** | Мéлкий |
| To exchange (foreign money) | **Abminyát** | Обменя́ть |
| Foreign currency | **Valyúta** | Валю́та |
| To change (large notes for smaller); to split | **Razminyát** | Разменя́ть |
| To sign the receipt | **Rasspissátsya** | Расписа́ться |

Where can I change some English (American) money?

**Gdyé mózhna abminyát angléeskiye (amirikánskiye) dyéngy?**

Где мо́жно обменя́ть англи́йские (америка́нские) де́ньги?

Where is the National Bank?

**Gdyé Gosbánk?**

Где Госуда́рственный банк (Госба́нк)?

Where is the nearest branch of the National Bank?

**Gdyé blizháyshe atdilyénye Gosbánka?**

Где ближа́йшее отделе́ние Госба́нка?

Can I change money at Intourist?

**Mózhna abminyát dyéngy v inturéestye?**

Мо́жно обменя́ть де́ньги в Интури́сте?

Can I change a traveller's cheque?

**Mózhna paluchéet dyéngy pa turéestskamu chéku?**

Мо́жно получи́ть де́ньги по тури́стскому че́ку?

Can you change English
(American) money?

**Mózhitye abminyát angléeskiye
(amirikánskiye) dyéngy?**
Мóжете обменя́ть англи́йские
(америка́нские) де́ньги?

Can you cash this cheque?

**Mózhitye aplateét état chek?**
Мóжете оплати́ть э́тот чек?

What is the official rate for
English (American) money?

**Kakóy afitsyálny kurss angléesky
(amirikánsky) valyúty?**
Како́й официа́льный курс
англи́йской (америка́нской)
валю́ты?

Where do I sign the receipt?

**Gdyé rasspissátsya?**
Где расписа́ться?

Can you give me 5 roubles' worth
of small notes and silver?

**Dáytye myélkye bilyéty ee
siribráh na pyát rubléy?**
Да́йте ме́лкие биле́ты и
серебра́ на пять рубле́й

Change this note please (i.e. split
it into smaller)

**Pazminyáytye état bilyét**
Разменя́йте э́тот биле́т

# Travel

## By train

Most long distance travel will be both organised and paid for in advance. Those tourists taking independent excursions inside the Soviet Union would be wise to get a porter to take them to their train. Just show him the ticket and remember that the charge for each piece of luggage is 30 kopecks.

Tea is served during the journey. You pay when you leave the train: it is 4 kopecks a glass and you can leave the money on the table in your compartment.

It is usual in the Soviet Union for men and women to travel in the same sleepers and to share cabins on ships. Presumably the attendant would try to transfer anyone who objected strongly to the arrangement.

The attendant keeps all tickets and gives them back, if they are needed, at the end of the journey.

## By car

You can hire a car at your hotel through Intourist; you must be accompanied by a guide, who will give you all the details you need to know concerning traffic regulations.

## The underground

Most major Soviet cities have underground systems and the Moscow line, with more than 100 stations, is not only a superb means of transport but is worth an hour or so's visit as a place of interest: some of the stations are fascinating.

The stations are marked by a large red M that is illuminated at night. You reach the platforms by putting a 5 kopeck coin into the automatic gates inside the entrance. (Any journey, regardless of distance, costs 5 kopecks.) If you have no change there are machines on all stations: you put in 10, 15 or 20 kopeck coins and receive the corresponding number of 5 kopeck coins. Banknotes can be changed at the cash desks.

The underground system in Moscow is very logical and plans in English can be bought.

During the journey the name of the station is announced at each stop and the name of the next station is also given.

On the train passengers are expected to give up their seats to invalids, elderly people and to children. Smoking and throwing litter are strictly forbidden.

The trains are very fast and very frequent (they come at 45 second intervals for most of the day). The underground operates from 6 am–1 am, and for longer periods on holidays.

## Bus, tram and trolleybus

Once again flat fares operate:   bus – 5 kopecks
trolleybus – 4 kopecks
tram – 3 kopecks

There are no conductors and the fare should be dropped into the boxes and a ticket torn off.

The buses and trolleybuses get very full on the most popular routes and although the driver is obliged to announce the stops it is often difficult to hear him and understand what he is saying.

If you do decide to travel by bus or trolleybus you will certainly have to join in the business of passing money or tickets along the bus to and from the ticket machine or the driver. You will be given money or tickets with the words: 'Piridaytye, pazhalusta', and you will repeat these words as you pass them on. The wise tourist never stands near the ticket machine!

In all forms of transport the following phrases are heard regularly, and visitors to the Soviet Union should know them.

Vi vikhóditye sicháss? (Are you getting out now?)
Vi vikhóditye na slyédushchy (astanófkye)? (Are you getting off at the next stop?)

The answer is either:

Da (skhazhú) (Yes),
or
Nyét (No) and you let the inquirer past you.

## By taxi

Taxis can be recognised by the black and white chequered band that runs along the body of the vehicle. The Russian 'For Hire' sign is a small green light at the top, right-hand side of the windscreen. If this light is on, the taxi may be hailed. Taxis are less expensive than in London, and are always available at large hotels. They can also be ordered in advance from the Service Bureau or from the desk-clerk in your hotel for about 20 kopecks.

## By boat and plane

Internal flights on Aeroflot are available through Intourist. You can sail down the Volga, but this must be arranged, as a holiday, in advance. In Moscow, Leningrad and Kiev you can take river trips by steamer or hydrofoil, which are both pleasant and inexpensive. These are *not* tourist excursions, but are principally an alternative form of public transport.

## By air

| | | |
|---|---|---|
| Air transport (communications) | **Vazdúshnaye sa-abschénye** | Воздýшное сообщéние |

| | | |
|---|---|---|
| Aeroplane | **Samalyót** | Самолёт |
| Jet aeroplane | **Riaktéevny samalyót** | Реакти́вный самолёт |
| Helicopter | **Virtalyót** | Вертолёт |
| Engine | **Matór** | Мото́р |
| Cabin | **Kabéena** | Каби́на |
| Cockpit | **Kabéena pilóta** | Каби́на пило́та |
| Wing | **Krillóh** | Крыло́ |
| Airways time-table | **Rasspissánye vazdúshnikh léeniy** | Расписа́ние возду́шных ли́ний |
| Passenger | **Passazhéer** | Пассажи́р |
| Air hostess | **Styuardéssa** | Стюарде́сса |
| Airport | **Aerapórt** | Аэропо́рт |
| Aerodrome | **Aeradróm** | Аэродро́м |
| To take off | **Vslitát** | Взлета́ть |
| To land | **Prizimlyátsya (dyélat passátku)** | Приземля́ться (де́лать поса́дку) |
| To fly | **Lityét** | Лете́ть |
| Gangway | **Trap** | Трап |
| Fuselage | **Fyusilázh** | Фюзеля́ж |
| Luggage compartment | **Bagázhnaye atdilyénye** | Бага́жное отделе́ние |
| Buffet | **Buffyét** | Буфе́т |
| Toilet (lavatory) | **Twalyét (ubórnaya)** | Туале́т (убо́рная) |
| Regular service | **Ryéyss** | Рейс |

What is the nearest way to the aerodrome? **Kakóy blizháyshy put k aeradrómy?**
Како́й ближа́йший путь к аэродро́му?

When does the Vienna plane leave? **Kagdá atpravlyáyitsya samalyót v Viénnu?**
Когда́ отправля́ется самолёт в Ве́ну?

The next plane doesn't go till one o'clock **Slyédushchy samalyót atpravlyáyitsya tólka f chass**
Сле́дующий самолёт отправля́ется то́лько в час

| | |
|---|---|
| The time-table is in the hall | **Rasspissánye nakhóditsya v zálye** |
| | Расписáние нахóдится в зáле |
| I should like to fly direct | **Ya bi khatyél lityét pryamím sa-abshchényem** |
| | Я бы хотéл летéть прямы́м сообщéнием |
| Without an intermediate landing | **Biz pramizhútachnay pasátky** |
| | Без промежу́точной посáдки |
| How many passengers does this plane take? | **Skólka passazhéeraf biryót état samalyót?** |
| | Скóлько пассажи́ров берёт э́тот самолёт? |
| This plane takes 50 passengers and has a crew of five | **État samalyót pirivózit pitdissyát passazhéeraf ee pyát chilovyék kamándy** |
| | Э́тот самолёт перевóзит пятьдеся́т пассажи́ров и пять человéк комáнды |
| Where will they put my luggage? | **Kudá pamistyát móy bagásh?** |
| | Кудá помéстя́т мой багáж? |
| In the luggage compartment | **V bagáznhom atdilyény** |
| | В багáжном отделéнии |
| The plane is just taxi-ing out of the hangar | **Samalyót kak pas sicháss vikhódit eez angára** |
| | Самолёт как раз сейчáс выхóдит из ангáра |
| Individual ventilation here | **Zdyés individuálnaya vintilyátseeya** |
| | Здесь индивидуáльная вентиля́ция |
| How high are we flying now? | **Na kakóy vissotyéh litéem tipyér?** |
| | На какóй высотé лети́м тепéрь? |
| The visibility is good (bad) | **Kharóshaya (plakháya) véedimast** |
| | Хорóшая (плохáя) ви́димость |

| | |
|---|---|
| That's an air pocket | **Éta vazdúshnaya yáma**<br>Это воздушная яма |
| It's good flying weather today | **Sivódnya kharóshaya lyótnaya pagóda**<br>Сегодня хорошая, лётная погода |
| It's not flying weather today | **Sivódnya nilyótnaya pagóda**<br>Сегодня нелётная погода |
| I can't stand flying very well | **Ya plókha pirinashú palyót**<br>Я плохо переношу полёт |
| I (she, he) feel(s) sick | **Mnyé (yey, yimú) durnóh**<br>Мне (ей, ему) дурно |
| I've gone deaf | **Ya aglókh (aglókhla)**<br>Я оглох (оглохла) |
| My ears are hurting | **Úshy balyát**<br>Уши болят |
| How long does the flight to Moscow take? | **Skólka vryéminy zanimáyit pirilyót da Maskvíy?**<br>Сколько времени занимает перелёт до Москвы? |
| Will there be stops at intermediate airfields? | **Búdut astanófky na pramizhútachnikh aeradrómakh?**<br>Будут остановки на промежуточных аэродромах? |
| Yes, there'll be two landings | **Da, búdut dvyé passátky**<br>Да, будут две посадки |
| The plane is just coming in to land | **Samalyót uzhéh prizimlyáitsya**<br>Самолёт уже приземляется |
| Regular services have now been established between London and Moscow | **Tipyér ustanóvliny rigulyárniye ryéyssy myézhdu Lóndanam ee Maskvóy**<br>Теперь установлены регулярные рейсы между Лондоном и Москвой |

# By rail

| | | |
|---|---|---|
| Station | **Vaksál** | Вокзал |

| | | |
|---|---|---|
| Ticket | **Bilyét** | Билéт |
| Reservation | **Platskárta** | Плацкáрта |
| Booking office | **Bilyétnaya kássa** | Билéтная кáсса |
| Price of a ticket (fare) | **Stóyimast bilyéta (tsináh prayézda)** | Стóимость билéта (ценá проéзда) |
| Period of validity of a ticket | **Srok gódnasty bilyéta** | Срок гóдности билéта |
| Return ticket | **Bilyét tudá ee abrátna** | Билéт тудá и обрáтно |
| Luggage | **Bagásh** | Багáж |
| Left luggage office | **Kámera khranyénya bagazhá** | Кáмера хранéния багажá |
| Luggage office | **Bagázhnaya kássa** | Багáжная кáсса |
| Receipt for luggage | **Bagázhnaya kvitántsya** | Багáжная квитáнция |
| Passenger | **Passazhéer** | Пассажи́р |
| Waiting room | **Zal dlyá passazhéeraf** | Зал для пассажи́ров |
| Lavatory (men's, women's) | **Twalyét (mushskóy, zhénsky)** | Туалéт (для мужчи́н, для жéнщин) |
| Enquiry office | **Správachnoye byuróh** | Спрáвочное бюрó |
| Lost Property office | **Byuróh náydinnikh vyeshchéy (byuróh nakhódak)** | Бюрó нáйденных вещéй (бюрó нахóдок) |
| Buffet, refreshment room | **Buffyét** | Буфéт |
| Station Master | **Nachálnik stánsty** | Начáльник стáнции |
| Train | **Póyezd** | Пóезд |
| Passenger train (slow) | **Passazhéersky póyezd** | Пассажи́рский пóезд |
| Express train | **Skóry póyezd** | Скóрый пóезд |
| Suburban train | **Preégaradny póyezd** | При́городный пóезд |
| Time-table | **Rasspissánye (dvizhénya) payezdóf** | Расписáние (движéния) поездóв |
| Arrival of trains | **Pribítye payesdóf** | Прибы́тие поездóв |
| Departure of trains | **Atpravlyénye payezdóf** | Отправлéние поездóв |

| Platform | **Perrón (platfórma)** | Перро́н (платфо́рма) |
|---|---|---|
| Coach | **Vagón** | Ваго́н |
| (Non)smoking coach | **Vagón dlyá (ni)ku-ryáshchikh** | Ваго́н для (не)ку-ря́щих |
| Sleeping coach, car | **Spálny vagón** | Спа́льный вагóн |
| Soft (hard) class coach | **Myákhky (zhóstky) vagón** | Мя́гкий (жёсткий) вагóн |
| Suitcase | **Chimadán** | Чемода́н |
| Trunk | **Sundúk** | Сунду́к |
| Porter | **Nasséelshchik** | Носи́льщик |
| Room for 'mother and baby' | **Kómnata mátiry ee ribyónka** | Ко́мната ма́тери и ребёнка |
| Through coach (train) | **Vagón (póyezd) primóva sa-abshchénya** | Ваго́н (пóезд) прямóго со-обще́ния |
| Dining car | **Vagón ristarán** | Вагóн-рестора́н |
| Luggage van | **Bagázhny vagón** | Бага́жный вагóн |
| Compartment | **Kupyéh** | Купé |
| Seat | **Myésta** | Ме́сто |
| Corner seat | **Uglavóye myésta** | Углово́е ме́сто |
| Place in sleeper | **Spálnaye myésta** | Спа́льное ме́сто |
| Guard | **Kandúktar** | Конду́ктор |
| Attendant | **Pravadnéek** | Проводни́к |
| Number of coach (seat, porter) | **Nómir vagóna (myésta, naséelshchika)** | Но́мер вагóна (ме́ста, носи́ль-щика) |
| Change (to change trains) | **Pirisátka (pirisázhivatsya)** | Переса́дка (пере-са́живаться) |
| Break of journey | **Astanófka** | Остано́вка |

## Booking office

| Where can I get a ticket? | **Gdyé mózhna paluchéet bilyét?** |
|---|---|
| | Где мо́жно получи́ть биле́т? |
| Is the office open? | **Atkríta kássa?** |
| | Откры́та ка́сса? |

| | |
|---|---|
| It's closed at the moment | **Sicháss zakríta** |
| | Сейча́с закры́та |
| It will open at two | **Atkróyitsya v dvá chassá** |
| | Откро́ется в два часа́ |
| It will open in 15 minutes | **Atkróyitsya chériz pitnátsat minút** |
| | Откро́ется че́рез пятна́дцать мину́т |
| A ticket to Leningrad | **Bilyét da Liningráda** |
| | Биле́т до Ленингра́да |
| A ticket for an express train | **Bilyét na skóry póyezd** |
| | Биле́т на ско́рый по́езд |
| I want a place in a sleeper | **Ya khachú spálnaye myésta** |
| | Я хочу́ спа́льное ме́сто |
| I want a seat in a soft (hard) class coach | **Ya khachú myésta f myákhkam (v zhóstkam) vagóne** |
| | Я хочу́ ме́сто в мя́гком (в жёстком) вагóне |
| I want a seat in a (non)smoking coach | **Ya khachú myésta v vagóne dlyá (ni)kuryáshchikh** |
| | Я хочу́ ме́сто в вагóне для (не)куря́щих |
| Can one get a return ticket? | **Mózhna paluchéet bilyét tudá ee abrátna?** |
| | Мо́жно получи́ть биле́т туда́ и обра́тно? |
| How much does the ticket (reservation) cost? | **Skólka stóyit bilyét (platskárta)?** |
| | Ско́лько сто́ит биле́т (плацка́рта)? |
| Is it a direct train? | **Éta primóy póyezd?** |
| | Это прямо́й по́езд? |
| Is there a train that does not involve a change? | **Yést póyezd biz pirisátky?** |
| | Есть по́езд без переса́дки? |
| You won't have to change | **U vass ni búdyit pirisátky** |
| | У вас не бу́дет переса́дки |
| When does the Moscow train go? | **Kagdá atkhódit póezd na Maskvú?** |
| | Когда́ отхо́дит по́езд на Москву́? |

| | |
|---|---|
| From which platform? | **S kakóy platfórmy?** |
| | С какóй платфóрмы? |
| What is the number of my coach? | **Kakóy nómir moyivó vagóna?** |
| | Какóй нóмер моегó вагóна? |
| What is the number of my seat? | **Kakóy nómir moyivó myésta?** |
| | Какóй нóмер моегó мéста? |
| How long is this ticket valid? | **Kakóy srok gódnasty étava bilyéta?** |
| | Какóй срок гóдности э́того билéта? |
| Can I break my journey (here)? | **Magú ya sdyélat astanófku f puteé (zdyés)?** |
| | Могý я сдéлать останóвку в путú (здесь)? |
| I missed that train | **Ya apazdál na état póyezd** |
| | Я опоздáл на э́тот пóезд |
| When is the next train? | **Kagdá búdyit slyédushchy póyezd?** |
| | Когдá бýдет слéдующий пóезд? |
| When does the last train go? | **Kagdá idyót passlyédniy póyezd?** |
| | Когдá идёт послéдний пóезд? |
| Where can I see a time-table? | **Gdyé mózhna véedit rasspissánye payezdóf?** |
| | Где мóжно вúдеть расписáние поездóв? |
| This is the summer time-table | **Éta lyétniye rasspissánye** |
| | Э́то лéтнее расписáние |

## Porter and luggage

| | |
|---|---|
| Where can I find a porter? | **Gdyé mózhna nayteé nasseélshchika?** |
| | Где мóжно найтú носúльщика? |
| Send (call) me a porter | **Pashleétye (pazaveétye) mnyé nasseélshchika** |
| | Пошлúте (позовúте) мне носúльщика |

| | |
|---|---|
| What is your number, porter? | **Kakóy vash nómir, nasséelshchik?**<br>Какóй ваш нóмер, носи́льщик? |
| I want to take these things into the carriage | **Éty vyéshchy ya khachú vzyát v vagón**<br>Э́ти вéщи я хочу́ взять в вагóн |
| This case is too big for the luggage rack | **État chimadán sléeshkam vileék dlyá bagázhnay pólky**<br>Э́тот чемодáн сли́шком вели́к для багáжной пóлки |
| Have this case registered (with declaration of value) | **Sdáytye chimadán v bagásh (s abyávlinnoy tsénnastyu)**<br>Сдáйте чемодáн в багáж (с объя́вленной цéнностью) |
| Where is the luggage office? | **Gdyé bagázhnaya kássa?**<br>Где багáжная кáсса? |
| Must I pay excess? | **Dólzhin ya daplatéet?**<br>Дóлжен я доплати́ть? |
| You haven't given me the luggage receipt | **Vi nyé dály mnyé (bagázhnay) kvitántsy**<br>Вы нé дали мне (багáжной) квитáнции |
| How soon does the train come in (go)? | **Kak skóra padadút (atkhódit) póyezd?**<br>Как скóро подаду́т (отхóдит) пóезд? |
| Can I get into the train now? | **Mózhna uzhéh sadéetsya f póyezd?**<br>Мóжно ужé сади́ться в пóезд? |
| In half an hour. The train is late. | **Chériz palchassáh. Póyezd apazdiváyit**<br>Чéрез полчасá. Пóезд опáздывает |
| You can wait in the passengers' waiting room (buffet) | **Vi mózhityе padazhdát v zále dlyá passazhéeraf (v buffyétye)**<br>Вы мóжете подождáть в зáле для пассажи́ров (в буфéте) |

I shall wait for you at the entrance to platform 4

**Ya búdu zhdát vass u vkhóda na platfórmu nómir chitírye**

Я бу́ду ждать вас у вхо́да на платфо́рму но́мер четы́ре

Please tell me where platform no. 4 is

**Skazhéetye, pazhálusta, gdyé platfórma nómir chitírye?**

Скажи́те, пожа́луйста, где платфо́рма но́мер четы́ре?

On the left, through the subway

**Nalyéva, chériz tunnyél**

Нале́во, че́рез тунне́ль

On the right (straight on)

**Napráva (pryáma)**

Напра́во (пря́мо)

Put the travelling bag, coat and this parcel on the rack

**Palazhéetye sakvoyázh, paltó ee état pakyét na syétku (na pólku)**

Положи́те саквоя́ж, пальто́ и э́тот паке́т на се́тку (на по́лку)

Put that trunk here

**Passtáftye état chimadán syudá**

Поста́вьте э́тот чемода́н сюда́

I am breaking my journey here

**Ya dyelayú zdyés astanófky**

Я де́лаю здесь остано́вку

Is there a Left Luggage office here?

**Yést zdyés kámera khranyénya bagazhá?**

Есть здесь ка́мера хране́ния багажа́?

I want to leave this

**Ya khachú zdát éta na khranyénye**

Я хочу́ сдать э́то на хране́ние

Its value is 330 roubles

**Tsénnast tréesta tréetsat rubléy**

Це́нность три́ста три́дцать рубле́й

You must write a label

**Vi dalzhnée napissát yarlík**

Вы должны́ написа́ть ярлы́к

*In the train*

Is this seat free? No, it's taken.

**Éta myésta svabódna? Nyét, zányita**

Э́то ме́сто свобо́дно? Нет, за́нято

All the seats here are taken

**Zdyés vsyé mistáh zányity**
Здесь все местá зáняты

In the next coach there are plenty
of empty seats

**F slyédushchem vagóne mnóga
svabódnikh myést**
В слéдующем вагóне мнóго
свобóдных мест

Excuse me, this is my seat.
I have the reservation

**Izvinéetye, éta mayóh myésta.
U minyá platskárta**
Извини́те, э́то моё мéсто.
У меня́ плацкáрта

I have the lower (upper) sleeping
berth

**U minyá néezhniye (vyérkhniye)
spálnaye myésta**
У меня́ ни́жнее (вéрхнее)
спáльное мéсто

May I open the window (door)?
It's very stuffy here

**Mózhna atkrít aknóh (dvyér)?
Zdyés óchin dúshna**
Мóжно откры́ть окнó (дверь)?
Здесь óчень дýшно

May I close the window (door)?
There's a draught

**Razrishéetye zakrít aknóh
(dvyér)? Óchin dúyit**
Разреши́те закры́ть окнó
(дверь)? Óчень дýет

Let me close (open) the window

**Pazvóltye, ya zakróyu (atkróyu)
aknóh**
Позвóльте, я закрóю (открóю)
окнó

Take down my suitcase, please

**Sniméetye, pazhálusta, móy
chimadán**
Сними́те, пожáлуйста, мой
чемодáн

Let me take your suitcase down

**Pazvóltye, ya snimú vam
chimadán**
Позвóльте, я снимý вам
чемодáн

Here is the guard

**Vot (glávny) kandúktar**
Вот (глáвный) кондýктор

He is inspecting tickets

**On praviryáyit bilyéty**

Он проверя́ет биле́ты

And this is the attendant of our coach

**A éta pravadnéek náshiva vagóna**

А э́то проводни́к на́шего ваго́на

What is the next station (stop)?

**Kakáya slyédushchaya stántsya (astanófka)?**

Кака́я сле́дующая ста́нция (остано́вка)?

When do we get there?

**Kagdá mi búdyim tam?**

Когда́ мы бу́дем там?

Is there a buffet there?

**Yést tam buffyét?**

Есть там буфе́т?

How long does the train stop?

**Skólka vryéminy búdyit stoyát póyezd?**

Ско́лько вре́мени бу́дет стоя́ть по́езд?

Tell me when I have to change

**Pridupridéetye minyá, kagdá búdyit pirisátka**

Предупреди́те меня́, когда́ бу́дет переса́дка!

I should like to change to soft class (a sleeping car)

**Ya khatyél bi piriytée f myákhky (spálny) vagón**

Я хоте́л бы перейти́ в мя́гкий (спа́льный) ваго́н

How much extra do I pay?

**Skólka náda daplatéet?**

Ско́лько на́до доплати́ть?

Attendant, help me to raise (lower) the upper berth

**Pravadnéek, pamagéetye padnyát (apustéet) spéenku**

Проводни́к, помоги́те подня́ть (опусти́ть) спи́нку

Give me another pillow and blanket

**Dáyte yishchóh padúshku ee adiyála**

Да́йте ещё поду́шку и одея́ло

Close the ventilator

**Zakróytye vintilyátar**

Закро́йте вентиля́тор

| | | |
|---|---|---|
| Switch on (off) the light | **Fklyucheétye (víklyucheetye) svyét** | Включи́те (вы́ключите) свет |
| Can you bring me some tea (mineral water)? | **Mózhitye prinisteé mnyé cháyu (minirálnuyu vódu)?** | Мо́жете принести́ мне ча́ю (минера́льную во́ду)? |
| Is the dining car at the front or the back of the train? | **Vagón ristarán v galavyéh eely v khvastyé póyezda?** | Ваго́н-рестора́н в голове́ или в хвосте́ по́езда? |
| Take my things to another coach (compartment) | **Pirinisseétye mayeé vyéshchy v drugóy vagón (v drugóye kupyéh)** | Перенеси́те мои́ ве́щи в друго́й ваго́н (в друго́е купе́) |
| Wake me at eight | **Razbudeétye minyá v vóssyim chassóf** | Разбуди́те меня́ в во́семь часо́в |
| When will you be making up the sleepers? | **Kagdá vi dadeéte bilyóh?** | Когда́ вы дади́те бельё? |

## By car

| | | |
|---|---|---|
| Motor-car | **Aftamabeél** | Автомоби́ль (маши́на) |
| Motor bus (coach) | **Aftóbuss** | Авто́бус |
| Motorist | **Aftamabileést** | Автомобили́ст |
| Driver | **Vadeétyil** | Води́тель |
| Engine | **Dvéegatyil (matór)** | Дви́гатель (мото́р) |
| Body | **Kúzaf** | Ку́зов |
| Bonnet | **Kapót** | Капо́т |
| Boot | **Bagázhnik** | Бага́жник |
| Wing | **Krillóh** | Крыло́ |
| Wheel | **Kolissóh** | Колесо́ |

| Tyre | **Shéena** | Ши́на |
| Accelerator | **Uckaréetyil (aksilirátor)** | Ускори́тель (акселера́тор) |
| Speedometer | **Spidómitr** | Спидо́метр |
| Brake | **Tórmas** | То́рмоз |
| Gear-lever | **Richák (piriklyu-chénya) piridách** | Рыча́г (переклю-че́ния) переда́ч |
| Gear-box | **Karópka piridách** | Коро́бка переда́ч |
| Steering wheel | **Rulivóye kalissóh (rul)** | Рулево́е колесо́ (руль) |
| Exhaust | **Vikhlapnáya trubá** | Выхлопна́я труба́ |
| Battery | **Bataréya** | Батаре́я |
| Starter | **Stártir** | Ста́ртер |
| Bumper | **Búffir** | Бу́фер |
| Motor-horn | **Aftamabéelny razhók** | Автомоби́льный рожо́к |
| Windscreen | **Piryédniye stiklóh** | Пере́днее стекло́ |
| Side-window | **Bakavóye stiklóh** | Боково́е стекло́ |
| Spare parts | **Zapasnéeye chásty** | Запасны́е ча́сти |
| Petrol station | **Binzazaprávachnaya (Zaprávachnaya kalónka)** | Бензозапра́вочная (Запра́вочная коло́нка) |
| Petrol (fuel) | **Binzéen (garyúchiye)** | Бензи́н (горю́чее) |
| Garage (for repairs) | **Garázh (dlyá pachéenak)** | Гара́ж (для почи́нок) |
| Pedal of the accelerator (brake, clutch) | **Pidál aksilirátara (tórmaza, stsiplyénya)** | Педа́ль акселера́-тора (то́рмоза, сцепле́ния) |
| To change gear | **Piriklyuchát piridáchu** | Переключа́ть переда́чу |
| To engage first (second, third) gear | **Fklyuchéet pyérvuyu (ftarúyu, tryétyu) piridáchu** | Включи́ть пе́рвую (втору́ю, тре́тью) переда́чу |
| To de-clutch | **Vízhat stsiplyénye** | Вы́жать сцепле́ние |
| Motorway | **Aftamagistrál, aftadaróga** | Автомагистра́ль, автодоро́га |
| Main (high) road | **Shosséy** | Шоссе́ |

| | | |
|---|---|---|
| By-road (unpaved) | **Prasyólak** | Просёлок |
| Road sign | **Dorózhny znak** | Доро́жный знак |
| Traffic rules (Highway Code) | **Právila yezdíy** | Пра́вила езды́ |
| Signpost | **Ukazátil darógy** | Указа́тель доро́ги |
| Motoring signals | **Signál aftamashéeny** | Сигна́л авто-маши́ны |
| To give a signal | **Davát signál** | Дава́ть сигна́л |
| Reduce (increase) speed | **Zamidlyát (uskaryát) khot** | Замедля́ть (уско-ря́ть) ход |
| to stop | **Astanávlivatsya** (*perf.* **astana-véetsya**) | Остана́вливаться (*perf.* остано-ви́ться) |
| Street | **Úlitsa** | У́лица |

Is this car yours?

**Éta mashéena vásha?**

Э́та маши́на ва́ша?

Have you a driving licence?

**Yést u vass razrishénye právit?**

Есть у вас разреше́ние пра́вить?

I am a traffic policeman

**Yá darózhny inspyéktar**

Я доро́жный инспе́ктор

What is your route?

**Kakóy vash marshrút?**

Како́й ваш маршру́т?

Where (from where) are you going?

**Kudá (atkúda) vi yéditye?**

Куда́ (отку́да) вы е́дете?

Shall we open the roof?

**Ni atkrít ly nam vyérkh?**

Не откры́ть ли нам верх?

It's getting hot

**Stanóvitsya zhárka**

Стано́вится жа́рко

Watch out for turnings

**Astarózhna na pavarótakh**

Осторо́жно на поворо́тах

Did you see the traffic lights?

**Vi zamyétily svitafór?**

Вы заме́тили светофо́р?

The policeman took our number

**Militsyanyér zapisál nash nómir**

Милиционе́р записа́л наш но́мер

We'll have to pay a fine

**Mi dalzhneé búdyim zaplateét shtraff**

Мы должны́ бу́дем заплати́ть штраф

Have you any spares with you?

**Yést u vass saboy zapasneéye chásty?**

Есть у вас с собо́й запасны́е ча́сти?

Shall I press the starter?

**Nazhát na stártir?**

Нажа́ть на ста́ртер?

Speed up!

**Uskaryáytye!**

Ускоря́йте!

Slow down!

**Zamidlyáytye khot!**

Замедля́йте ход!

This is a one-way road

**Daróga tólka v adnóm napravlyényi**

Доро́га то́лько в одно́м направле́нии

Speed limit 80 kilometres

**Skórast ni bólshye vosmeédissyaty kilamyétraf**

Ско́рость не бо́льше восьми́десяти киломе́тров

Caution: crossroads

**Astarózhna: pirikryóstak**

Осторо́жно: перекрёсток

Main road (motorway) ahead

**Glávnaya úlitsa (magistrál) fpirideé**

Гла́вная у́лица (магистра́ль) впереди́

Road repairs (in town or country)

**Pacheénka úlitsy (darógy)**

Почи́нка у́лицы (доро́ги)

Detour (diversion)

**Abyézd**

Объе́зд

Level crossing

**Zhilyeznadarózhny piriyézd**

Железнодоро́жный перее́зд

You must switch on the headlights

**Vi dalzhneé zazhéch fáry**

Вы должны́ зажéчь фа́ры

We are going down-hill

**Mi yédim pód-garu**

Мы éдем под го́ру

| Where can I park the car? | **Gdyé ya magú pastávit mashéenu?** |
| | Где я могу́ поста́вить маши́ну? |
| Where can I get the car repaired? | **Gdyé ya magú zdát v rimónt mashéenu?** |
| | Где я могу́ сдать в ремо́нт маши́ну? |
| I've had a collision | **U minyá bwíla stalknavyénye** |
| | У меня́ бы́ло столкнове́ние |
| Where is the nearest petrol station? | **Gdyé blizháyshaya zaprávachnaya kalónka?** |
| | Где ближа́йшая запра́вочная коло́нка? |
| I need the tank filled and some air in the tyres | **Mnyé náda napólnit bak ee nadút shéeny** |
| | Мне на́до напо́лнить бак и наду́ть ши́ны |
| I've had an accident on the road | **U minyá bwilá avárya f putée** |
| | У меня́ была́ ава́рия в пути́ |
| I've got a burst tyre | **U minyá lópnula shéena** |
| | У меня́ ло́пнула ши́на |
| My engine has broken down | **U minyá ispórtilsya matór** |
| | У меня́ испо́ртился мото́р |
| The bumper is damaged | **Pavrizhdyón búffir** |
| | Повреждён бу́фер |
| What make of car is this? | **Kakóy márky état aftamabéel?** |
| | Како́й ма́рки э́тот автомоби́ль? |
| How much petrol does it take? | **Skólka biryót benzéena?** |
| | Ско́лько берёт бензи́на? |

## By boat

| Port, harbour | **Port** | Порт |
| Quay, jetty | **Préestan** | Пристань |
| Steamship company | **Parakhódnaye óbshchistva** | Парохо́дное о́бщество |
| Passenger ship | **Passazhéersky parakhót** | Пассажи́рский парохо́д |

| | | |
|---|---|---|
| Single-class ship | **Adnaklássny passazhéersky parakhót** | Однокла́ссный пассажи́рский парохо́д |
| First (second, third) class | **Pyérvy (ftaróy, tryéty) klass** | Пе́рвый (второ́й, тре́тий) класс |
| Tourist class | **Turéestsky klass** | Тури́стский класс |
| Passage, crossing | **Piriyézd** | Перее́зд |
| Gangway | **Skhódny** | Схо́дни |
| Funnel | **Trubá** | Труба́ |
| Porthole | **Ilyuminátor** | Иллюмина́тор |
| Railings | **Pireela** | Пери́ла |
| Dining saloon | **Stalóvaya** | Столо́вая |
| Smoking room | **Kuréetilnaya (kómnata)** | Кури́тельная (ко́мната) |
| Cabin | **Kayúta** | Каю́та |
| Deck | **Páluba** | Па́луба |
| Deck-chair | **Skladnóye kryésla** | Складно́е кре́сло |
| Life-boat | **Spassátilnaya lódka** | Спаса́тельная ло́дка |
| Life-belt | **Spassátilny póyass** | Спаса́тельный по́яс |
| Passenger | **Passazhéer** | Пассажи́р |
| Seasickness | **Marskáya balyézn** | Морска́я боле́знь |
| Crew | **Kamánda** | Кома́нда |
| Captain | **Kapitán** | Капита́н |
| Sailor | **Matróss** | Матро́с |
| Purser | **Kaznachéy** | Казначе́й |
| To book a passage | **Vzyát bilyét** | Взять биле́т |
| To embark | **Sadéetsya na parakhót** | Сади́ться на парохо́д |
| To disembark | **Skhadéet c parakhóda** | Сходи́ть с парохо́да |

Have you booked your passage? **Vi vzyály bilyét na parakhót?**
Вы взя́ли биле́т на парохо́д?

Which route did you choose? **Kakóy put vi izbrály?**
Како́й путь вы избра́ли?

When does the boat sail? **Kagdá atkhódit parakhót?**
Когда́ отхо́дит парохо́д?

| | |
|---|---|
| I am going first (second) class | **Ya yédu pyérvim (ftarím) klássam**<br>Я éду пéрвым (вторьým) клáссом |
| Where does it put in? | **Gdyé on astanávlivayitsya f putée?**<br>Где он останáвливается в путú? |
| How long does it stay at Stockholm? | **Skólka on búdit stoyát f Stockhólmye?**<br>Скóлько он бýдет стоя́ть в Стокгóльме? |
| Do you want to go ashore there and look at the city? | **Vi khatéetye saytée tam na byérig, pasmatryét górat?**<br>Вы хотúте сойтú там на бéрег, посмотрéть гóрод? |
| Where can I see a time-table? | **Gdyé mózhna véedit rasspissánye?**<br>Где мóжно вúдеть расписáние? |
| Is there an excursion for the passengers? | **Yést ekskúrsiya dlyá passazhéeraf?**<br>Есть экскýрсия для пассажúров? |
| Where is my cabin? | **Gdyé mayáh kayúta?**<br>Где моя́ каю́та? |
| May I take the lower (upper) berth? | **Magú ya zanyát néezhnyuyu (vyérkhnyuyu) kóyku?**<br>Могý я заня́ть нúжнюю (вéрхнюю) кóйку? |
| Where can I get a deck-chair? | **Gdyé ya magú paluchéet skladnóye kryésla?**<br>Где я могý получúть складнóе крéсло? |
| Can I go on the top deck? | **Mózhna praytée na vyérkhnyuyu pálubu?**<br>Мóжно пройтú на вéрхнюю пáлубу? |

| | |
|---|---|
| May I take this chair? | **Mózhna vzyát éta kryésla?**<br>Мо́жно взять э́то кре́сло? |
| May I look at the engine-room? | **Mózhna pasmatryét masheénaye**<br>**atdilyénye?**<br>Мо́жно посмотре́ть маши́нное<br>отделе́ние? |
| Send me the stewardess | **Pashleétye mnyé górnichnuyu**<br>Пошли́те мне го́рничную |
| Can you bring me (us) some tea<br>  to the cabin?<br>    soda water?<br>    my (our) breakfast? | **Mózhitye prinesteé mnyé (nam)**<br>**f kayútu: cháyu? sódavay**<br>**vadeé? móy (nash) záftrak?**<br>Мо́жете принести́ мне (нам)<br>в каю́ту: ча́ю? со́довой<br>воды́? мой (наш) за́втрак? |
| Is there a doctor on board? | **Yést na parakhódye vrach?**<br>Есть на парохо́де врач? |
| My wife is ill | **Moyéy zhinyéh plókha**<br>Мое́й жене́ пло́хо |
| I feel seasick | **Minyá ukachála**<br>Меня́ укача́ло |
| Are you seasick? | **Vass ni ukáchivayit?**<br>Вас не ука́чивает? |
| Are you a good (bad) sailor? | **Vi kharóshy (plakhóy) maryák?**<br>Вы хоро́ший (плохо́й) моря́к? |
| The sea is very rough (calm) | **Mórye óchin búrnaye (teékhaye)**<br>Мо́ре о́чень бу́рное (ти́хое) |
| Visibility is bad | **Veédimost plakháya**<br>Ви́димость плоха́я |
| The fog-horn is sounding | **Gudéet siryéna**<br>Гуди́т сире́на |
| Where can I hand in a radio-<br>  telegram? | **Gdyé ya magú zdát radio-**<br>**telegrámu?**<br>Где я могу́ сдать ра́дио-<br>телегра́мму? |
| In the wireless-operator's cabin | **F kayútye radeésta**<br>В каю́те ради́ста |

| | | |
|---|---|---|
| Have your passports and tickets ready | **Preegatóftye passpartáh ee bilyéty** | |
| | Приготóвьте паспортá и билéты | |
| You can see the coast | **Véedin byérig** | |
| | Вѝден бéрег | |
| We shall soon tie up | **Mi skóra prichálim** | |
| | Мы скóро причáлим | |
| A sailor will take your things on shore (on to the quay) | **Matróss snissyót váshy vyéshchy na byérig (na preéstan)** | |
| | Матрóс снесёт вáши вéщи на бéрег (на прѝстань) | |

## Bicycle and motor-cycle

| Bicycle | **Vilasipyét** | Велосипéд |
|---|---|---|
| Moped | **Motavilosipyét** | Мотовелосипéд |
| Motor-cycle | **Motatseékl** | Мотоцѝкл |
| Handlebars | **Rul** | Руль |
| Saddle | **Sidlóh** | Седлó |
| Pedal | **Pidál** | Педáль |
| Bell | **Zvanók** | Звонóк |
| Frame | **Ráma** | Рáма |
| Brake | **Tórmaz** | Тóрмоз |
| Pump | **Nassóss** | Насóс |
| Tool-bag | **Mishók dlyá instrumyéntaf** | Мешóк для инструмéнтов |

| | | |
|---|---|---|
| I am fond of cycling | **Yá lyublyú katátsya na vilasipyédye** | |
| | Я люблю́ катáться на велосипéде | |
| Are your brakes in order? | **V ispráfnasty ly vash tórmas?** | |
| | В испрáвности ли ваш тóрмоз? | |
| Yes, but the chain is a bit loose | **Da, no tsep nyéskalka aslábla** | |
| | Да, но цепь нéсколько ослáбла | |

You are riding on the pavement; you will have to pay a fine

**Vi yédyetye pa tratuáru, vam pridyótsya zaplateét shtraff**

Вы е́дете тротуа́ру, вам придётся заплати́ть штраф

I shall have to push my bicycle up-hill

**Mnyé pridyótsya pishkóm tashcheét móy vilasipyéd v góru**

Мне придётся пешко́м тащи́ть мой велосипе́д в го́ру

I must blow my tyres up

**Yá dólzhen nakachát (nadút) sheény**

Я до́лжен накача́ть (наду́ть) ши́ны

I have a puncture in my rear tyre; I must mend it

**U minyá v zádniy sheéney prakól, pridyótsya pachineét**

У меня́ в за́дней ши́не проко́л, придётся почини́ть

Can you lend me a pump?

**Mózhitye vi adalzheét mnyé nassóss?**

Мо́жете вы одолжи́ть мне насо́с?

I have lost my bicycle spanner

**Yá patiryál klyúch at vilasipyéda**

Я потеря́л ключ от велосипе́да

Put your bicycle in the shed

**Pastáftye vash vilasipyéd pad navyéss**

Поста́вьте ваш велосипе́д под наве́с

No cycling!

**Vilasipyédnaya yezdáh zaprishchináh!**

Велосипе́дная езда́ запрещена́!

# At the Hotel

On every floor in the hotel there is an attendant, the 'dizhúrnaya', who keeps the keys etc. This attendant can be helpful; for example she will make cups of tea at any time, call taxis, show you where you can press your clothes etc. Do not hesitate to ask for her assistance.

Visitors to the Soviet Union can 'use' their hotels to save time and, often, money. All large hotels have post offices where there are no queues so that letters, cards and parcels can be sent quickly and easily. It is cheap and easy to send books home by post: remember that the service of the Soviet Union Post Office includes packing so you need do nothing except address the parcel and pay.

*The hotel service bureau* (byuroh absluzhivanya; бюро обслуживание) can be very helpful. Here you can ask for theatre tickets, advice about shopping, weather forecasts etc.

| Hotel, inn | Gastéenitsa | Гости́ница |
|---|---|---|
| Single room | Kómnata (nómir) dlyá advanóh | Ко́мната (но́мер) для одного́ |
| Double room | Kómnata dlyá dvayéekh | Ко́мната для двои́х |
| Reception desk, office | Kantóra | Конто́ра |
| Lounge | Vistibyúl | Вестибю́ль |
| Dining-room | Stalóvaya (ristarán, buffyét, bar) | Столо́вая (рестора́н, буфе́т, бар) |
| Bathroom | Vánnaya (kómnata) | Ва́нная (ко́мната) |
| Lift | Léeft | Лифт |
| Gentlemen's lavatory | Muzhskóy twalyét | Мужско́й туале́т |

| Ladies' lavatory | **Zhénsky twalyét** | Жéнский туалéт |
|---|---|---|
| Bell | **Zvanók** | Звонóк |
| Chambermaid | **Górnichnaya** | Гóрничная |
| Lift attendant | **Leeftyór** | Лифтёр |
| Waiter | **Afitsiánt** | Официáнт |
| Head waiter | **Stárshy afitsiánt** | Стáрший официáнт |
| Waitress | **Afitsiántka** | Официáнтка |
| Porter | **Shveytsár** | Швейцáр |
| Manager | **Zavyéduyushchy (Diryéktor)** | Завéдующий (Дирéктор) |
| Receptionist | **Dizhúrny [administrátor]** | Дежýрный администрáтор |
| Service bureau | **Byuróh abslúzhivanya** | Бюрó обслýживание |

At which hotel are you staying?

**F kakóy gasteénitse vi astanaveélis?**

В какóй гостúнице вы остановúлись?

The service is good (bad)

**Abslúzhivanye kharósheye (plakhóye)**

Обслýживание хорóшее (плохóе)

There is central heating, and hot and cold water in the rooms

**Yést tsintrálnaye ataplyénye ee garyáchaya ee khalódnaya vadá v nomirákh**

Есть центрáльное отоплéние и горячая и холóдная водá в номерáх

The food is good and plentiful

**Kórmyit kharashóh ee abeélna**

Кóрмят хорошó и обúльно

The cooking is excellent

**Gatóvyit prikrásna**

Готóвят прекрáсно

I ordered a room with a bath

**Ya zakazál kómnatu s vánnoy**

Я заказáл кóмнату с вáнной

Have you reserved me a room?

**Vi astávily mnyé kómnatu?**

Вы остáвили мне кóмнату?

I shall not take meals in the hotel

**Ya ni búdu pitátsya v gasteénitse**

Я не бу́ду пита́ться в гости́нице

Can I have breakfast in my room?

**Magú ya paluchát útrinny záftrak u sibyáh f komnátye?**

Могу́ я получа́ть у́тренний за́втрак у себя́ в ко́мнате?

Enter your name and address in the visitors' book

**Napisheétye váshe eémya ee ádriss f kneégye dlyá pri-yezháyushchikh**

Напиши́те ва́ше и́мя и а́дрес в кни́ге для приезжа́ющих

How long do you intend to stay?

**Kak dólga vi namyériny astavátsya?**

Как до́лго вы наме́рены остава́ться?

Here is your key

**Vot klyúch ot váshey kómnaty**

Вот ключ от ва́шей ко́мнаты

The lift boy will take your luggage up

**Leeftyór padneémit vash bagásh**

Лифтёр подни́мет ваш бага́ж

We need two adjoining rooms.

**Nam núzhin nómir eez dvúkh kómnat**

Нам ну́жен но́мер из двух ко́мнат

I need a room with two beds

**Mnyé núzhin nómir s dvumyáh kravátamy**

Мне ну́жен но́мер с двумя́ крова́тами

I need a big room

**Mnyé nuzhnáh balsháya kómnata**

Мне нужна́ больша́я ко́мната

This room is too small (dark)

**État nómir sleéshkam mal (tyómny)**

Э́тот но́мер сли́шком мал (тёмный)

Have you a room facing the street (courtyard)?

**Yést u vass nómir na úlitsu (v dvór)**

Есть у вас но́мер на у́лицу (во двор)?

| | |
|---|---|
| Won't it be too cold (hot) here? | **Zdyés ni búdit sleéshkam khóladna (zhárka)?** |
| | Здесь не бу́дет сли́шком хо́лодно (жа́рко)? |
| What floor? | **Na kakóm etazhéy?** |
| | На како́м этаже́? |
| I'll take this room (these rooms) | **Yá vazmú étu kómnatu (éty kómnaty)** |
| | Я возьму́ э́ту ко́мнату (э́ти ко́мнаты) |
| What is its number? | **Kakóy yiyóh nómir?** |
| | Како́й её но́мер? |
| I should like another blanket or quilt | **Yá bi khatyél paluchéet yishchóh adnóh shirstyinóye éely vátnaye adiyála** |
| | Я бы хоте́л получи́ть ещё одно́ шерстяно́е и́ли ва́тное одея́ло |
| Give me another towel and some soap | **Dáytye mnyé yishchóh adnóh palatyéntsa ee mwíla** |
| | Да́йте мне ещё одно́ полоте́нце и мы́ло |
| Can you wake me tomorrow morning at six? | **Mózhitye vi minyá razbudéet záftra útram f shést chassóf?** |
| | Мо́жете вы меня́ разбуди́ть за́втра у́тром в шесть часо́в? |
| Send the waiter | **Pashléetye mnyé afitsyánta** |
| | Пошли́те мне официа́нта |
| Can I have breakfast at eight? | **Mózhna záftrakat v vóssyim chassóf?** |
| | Мо́жно за́втракать в во́семь часо́в? |
| Bring the menu | **Prinisséetye minyú** |
| | Принеси́те меню́ |
| Take this away | **Ubiréetye éta** |
| | Убери́те э́то |

Leave this here

**Astáftye éta zdyés**

Оста́вьте э́то здесь

Clean my suit (dress, shoes)

**Pacheéstitye móy kastyúm (mayóh plátye, moyeé bashmakeé)**

Почи́стите мой костю́м (моё пла́тье, мои́ башмаки́)

Can you get this suit pressed?

**Mózhna atdát kastyúm atyúzhit?**

Мо́жно отда́ть костю́м отю́жить?

I'd like a bath (shower)

**Yá khachú prinyát vánnu (dush)**

Я хочу́ приня́ть ва́нну (душ)

Is there an empty bathroom?

**Yést tipyér svabódnaya vánnaya?**

Есть тепе́рь свобо́дная ва́нная?

When will the water be hot?

**Kagdá búdit garyáchaya vodá?**

Когда́ бу́дет горя́чая вода́?

Thank you. Don't trouble

**Spasseéba, ni bispakóytyes**

Спаси́бо. Не беспоко́йтесь

I've forgotten my razor

**Yá zabwíl svayú breétvu**

Я забы́л свою́ бри́тву

Is there a barber in the hotel?

**Yést ly pri gasteénitse parik-mákhirskaya?**

Éсть-ли при гости́нице парик-ма́херская?

Where did you put my brush and comb?

**Kudá vi palazheély mayú shchótku ee gribyónku?**

Куда́ вы положи́ли мою́ щётку и гребёнку?

I want to send some things to the laundry

**Yá khatyél bi atdát kóye-shto f steérku**

Я хоте́л бы отда́ть ко́е-что в сти́рку

When will the washing be ready?

**Kagdá bilyóh búdit gatóva?**

Когда́ бельё бу́дет гото́во?

The laundry list

**Speéssak bilyáh dlyá steérky**

Спи́сок белья́ для сти́рки

| | |
|---|---|
| Four white shirts | **Chitírye byélikh rubáshky** |
| | Четы́ре бе́лых руба́шки |
| Three coloured shirts | **Trée tsvitníkh rubáshky** |
| | Три цветны́х руба́шки |
| Two vests | **Dvyé fufáyky** |
| | Две фуфа́йки |
| Two pairs of pants | **Dvyé páry kalsón** |
| | Две па́ры кальсо́н |
| One pair of pyjamas | **Adnáh pizháma** |
| | Одна́ пижа́ма |
| One nightdress | **Adnáh nachnáya rubáshka** |
| | Одна́ ночна́я руба́шка |
| Five pairs of socks (stockings) | **Pyát par naskóf (chulók)** |
| | Пять пар носко́в (чуло́к) |
| One blouse | **Adnáh blúska** |
| | Одна́ блу́зка |
| One linen dress | **Adnóh palatnyánaye plátye** |
| | Одно́ полотня́ное пла́тье |
| Aren't there any letters for me? | **Nyét ly mnyé péessyim?** |
| | Нет ли мне пи́сем? |
| Has anybody asked for me? | **Niktó minyá ni spráshival?** |
| | Никто́ меня́ не спра́шивал? |
| He (she) didn't give his (her) name? | **On (Anáh) ni skazál (a) svayevóñ éeminy?** |
| | Он (она́) не сказа́л(а) своего́ и́мени? |
| He said he would call again this evening (tomorrow morning) | **On skazál, shto zaydyót apyát vyéchiram (záftra útram)** |
| | Он сказа́л, что зайдёт опя́ть ве́чером (за́втра у́тром) |
| He left you a note (his phone number) | **On astávil vam zapéesku (nómir svoyevóh tilifóna)** |
| | Он оста́вил вам запи́ску (но́мер своего́ телефо́на) |
| What time did he come? | **F katóram chassú on prikhadéel?** |
| | В кото́ром часу́ он приходи́л? |

| | |
|---|---|
| I'm waiting for somebody | **Yá zhdú adnavóh grazhdaneéena (adnú grazhdánku)**<br>Я жду́ одного́ граждани́на (одну́ гражда́нку) |
| Say that I shall be back soon | **Skazheétye, shto yá skóra virnúss**<br>Скажи́те, что я ско́ро верну́сь |
| Ask them to wait for me | **Paprasseétye padazhdát minyá**<br>Попроси́те подожда́ть меня́ |
| I'm going out for the whole day (till evening) | **Yá uyezháyu na tsély dyén (da vyéchira)**<br>Я уезжа́ю на це́лый день (до ве́чера) |
| We are leaving tomorrow (this evening) | **Mi uyezháyim záftra (sivódnya vyéchiram)**<br>Мыуезжа́ем за́втра (сего́дня ве́чером) |
| Make up my bill please | **Prigatóftye shchót, pazhálusta**<br>Пригото́вьте счёт, пожа́луйста |
| Send my letters on to this address | **Péessma na mayóh éemya pirisiláytye pa étamu ádrissu**<br>Пи́сьма на моё и́мя пересыла́йте по э́тому а́дресу |
| There's a slight error in the account | **F shchótye yést málinkaya asheéebka**<br>В счёте есть ма́ленькая оши́бка |
| Thank you. Everything was very nice | **Spaseéeba. Vsyóh bwíla óchin kharashóh**<br>Спаси́бо. Всё бы́ло о́чень хорошо́ |
| Call a taxi | **Pazaveétye takseé**<br>Позови́те такси́ |

## The town

| Town, City | **Górat** | Город |
|---|---|---|
| Capital | **Staléetsa** | Столица |
| Suburb | **Préegarat** | Пригород |
| Outskirts | **Akráyna** | Окраина |
| Square | **Plóshchat** | Площадь |
| Street | **Úlitsa** | Улица |
| Main street | **Glávnaya úlitsa** | Главная улица |
| Side street | **Piriúlak** | Переулок |
| Corner | **Úgal** | Угол |
| Cross roads | **Pirikryóstak** | Перекрёсток |
| Traffic lights | **Svitafór** | Светофор |
| Pedestrian crossing | **Pirikhót** | Переход |
| Roadway | **Mastaváya** | Мостовая |
| Pavement | **Tratwár, panyél** | Тротуар, панель |
| Garden | **Sát** | Сад |
| Park | **Párk** | Парк |
| Garden in a square | **Skvyér** | Сквер |
| Bridge | **Mosst** | Мост |
| Cemetery | **Kládbishche** | Кладбище |
| Building | **Zdánye** | Здание |
| Hospital (health centre) | **Balnéetsa (polycléenika)** | Больница (поликлиника) |
| Town Hall | **Garadskóy Savyét** | Городской Совет |
| Post office | **Pachtóvaye atdilyénye (póchta)** | Почтовое отделение (почта) |
| Police station | **Atdilyénye miléetsiy** | Отделение милиции |
| Policeman | **Militsyanyér** | Милиционер |
| Public library | **Garadskáya bibliatyéka** | Городская библиотека |

| Theatre | **Tiátr** | Теáтр |
|---|---|---|
| Cinema | **Kéenotiatr** | Кинотеáтр |
| School | **Shkóla** | Шкóла |
| University | **Universityét** | Университéт |
| Church | **Tsérkof** | Цéрковь |
| Cathedral | **Sabór** | Собóр |
| Monastery | **Manastíyr (lávra)** | Монастырь (лáвра) |
| Fire station | **Pazhárnaya (chasst)** | Пожáрная (часть) |
| Block of flats | **Dom kvartéer** | Дом квартир |
|  | **(zhilóy dom)** | (жилóй дом) |
| Café | **Kafé** | Кафé |
| Restaurant | **Ristarán** | Ресторáн |
| Club | **Klup** | Клуб |
| Museum | **Muzyéy** | Музéй |
| Art gallery | **Kartéennaya** | Картинная |
|  | **galliryéya** | галерéя |
| Monument | **Pámyatrik** | Пáмятник |
| Palace | **Dvoryéts** | Дворéц |
| Planetarium | **Planitáriy** | Планетáрий |
| Shop | **Magazéen** | Магазин |
| Department store | **Univermág** | Универмáг |
| Shop window | **Vitréena** | Витрина |
| Pedestrian | **Pishikhót** | Пешехóд |
| Underground | **Mitróh** | Метрó |
| Underground station | **Stántsiya mitróh** | Стáнция метрó |
| Tram car | **Tramváy** | Трамвáй |
| Omnibus | **Aftóbuss** | Автóбус |
| Trolleybus | **Trallyéybuss** | Троллéйбус |
| Stopping place | **Astanófka** | Останóвка |
| Terminus | **Kanyéchnaya** | Конéчная стáнция |
|  | **stántsiya** |  |
| Taxi | **Taksée** | Такси |
| Taxi rank | **Stayánka taksée** | Стоянка такси |
| Lorry | **Gruzavéek** | Грузовик |

Is it far from here to the main street?

**Dalikóh atsyúda da glávnay úlitsy?**
Далекó отсю́да до глáвной у́лицы?

Ten minutes' walk (ride)

**Dyéssyat minút khadbíy (yezdíy)**
Дéсять минýт ходьбы́ (езды́)

What is the nearest way to the cathedral?

**Kakóy blizháyshiy put k sabóru?**
Какóй ближáйший путь к собóру?

I've lost my way

**Yá zbéelsya s darógy**
Я сби́лся с дорóги

Can you tell me please, how to get to the theatre?

**Skazhéetye, pazhálusta, kak praytée (prayékhot) k tiátru?**
Скажи́те, пожáлуйста, как пройти́ (проéхать) к теáтру?

Second turning to the right (left)

**Ftaróy pavarót napráva (nalyéva)**
Вторóй поворóт напрáво (налéво)

Go (drive) straight on

**Idéetye (payezháytye) pryáma**
Иди́те (поезжáйте) пря́мо

The stop is round the corner (on the opposite side, on the corner)

**Astanófka za uglóm (na drugóy staranyéh, na uglú)**
Останóвка за углóм (на другóй сторонé, на углý)

Don't push

**Ni talkáytyes**
Не толкáйтесь

Move along the car, please

**Prakhadéetye fpiryót, pazhálusta**
Проходи́те вперёд, пожáлуйста

Keep a gangway

**Astáftye prakhót**
Остáвьте прохóд

You didn't give me my change

**Vi né daly mnyé sdáchy**
Вы нé дали мне сдáчи

I've lost my ticket

**Yá patiryál svóy bilyét**
Я потеря́л свой билéт

Don't get off while the bus is moving

**Ni skhadéetye (slizáytye) na khadú**
Не сходи́те (слезáйте) на ходý

| | |
|---|---|
| When does the last tube train go? | **Kagdá atkhódit paslyédny póyezd mitróh?**<br>Когда́ отхо́дит после́дний по́езд метро́? |
| Take a ticket from the machine | **Biréetye bilyét eez aftamáta**<br>Бери́те биле́т из автома́та |
| Put a 20-kopeck piece in the slot | **Apustéetye manyétu v dvátsat kapyéyek**<br>Опусти́ть моне́ту в два́дцать копе́ек |
| The ticket is valid for three days | **Bilyét gódyin tróyeh sútak**<br>Биле́т го́ден тро́е су́ток |
| Do I get out here? | **Mnyé zdyés skhadéet?**<br>Мне здесь сходи́ть? |
| Where should I get off? | **Gdyé yá dólzhin saytée (slyézt)?**<br>Где я до́лжен сойти́ (слезть)? |
| Where is there a taxi rank? | **Gdyé zdyés stoyánka taksée?**<br>Где здесь стоя́нка такси́? |
| Taxi! Are you free? | **Taksée! Vi svabódny?**<br>Такси́! Вы свобо́дны? |
| Drive to the Bolshoi theatre | **Payezháytye v Balshóy tiátr**<br>Поезжа́йте в Большо́й теа́тр |
| I want to drive round the town | **Yá khachú prayékhat pa góradu**<br>Я хочу́ прое́хать по го́роду |
| I should like to see the old buildings and streets | **Yá khatyél bi uvéedit stáriye damáh ee úlitsy**<br>Я хоте́л бы уви́деть ста́рые дома́ и у́лицы |
| How much would that cost per hour? | **Skólka éta mózhit stóyit f chass?**<br>Ско́лько э́то мо́жет сто́ить в час? |
| No through road | **Nyét prayézda**<br>Нет прое́зда |
| Closed to pedestrians | **Dlyá pishikhódaf zakríta**<br>Для пешехо́дов закры́то |

Wait for the green light before crossing

**Nilzyá pirikhadéet do zilyónava signála**

Нельзя́ переходи́ть до зелёного сигна́ла

No admittance

**Fkhód zaprishcháyitsya**

Вход запреща́ется

What do you advise me to see today?

**Shto vi savyétuyitye mnyé pasmatryét sivódnya?**

Что вы сове́туете мне посмотре́ть сего́дня?

I have only one free day

**U minyá svabódin tólka adéen dyén**

У меня́ свобо́ден то́лько оди́н день

How do I get there?

**Kak tudá dayékhat?**

Как туда́ дое́хать?

Where can I get a taxi?

**Gdyé mózhna dastát taksée?**

Где мо́жно доста́ть такси́?

At what time does the museum (gallery) open?

**F kakóy vryémya muzyéy (galliryéya) atkrít (atkríta)?**

В како́е вре́мя музе́й (галере́я) откры́т (откры́та)?

On what days (on Sunday too)?

**Pa kakéem dnyam (v vaskrisyénye tózhe)?**

По каки́м дням (в воскресе́нье то́же)?

How much does it cost to get in?

**Skólka stóyit fkhót?**

Ско́лько сто́ит вход?

Are individual visits to the Kremlin allowed?

**Razrisháyutsya adinóchniye pasishchénya Krimlyáh?**

Разреша́ются одино́чные посеще́ния Кремля́?

Who arranges party visits?

**Kto arganizúyit grúpavaye pasishchénya?**

Кто организу́ет гру́пповое посеще́ние?

I advise you to go to the National
Library; to the Exhibition of
Soviet Artists, to the Zoo

**Savyétuyu vam payteé v gassudár-
stvinnuyu Bibliatyéku, na
vístafku karteén savyétskikh
khudóznikaf, v zoapárk**

Советую вам пойти в Государ-
ственную библиотеку, на
Выставку картин советских
художников, в Зоопарк

It would be best for you to join
some tour or other

**Vam lúchshe prisayedineétsya
k kakóy-nibut ekskúrsiy**

Вам лучше присоединиться
к какой-нибудь экскурсии

## A tour

What tours are there?

**Kakéeye yést ekskúrsiy?**

Какие есть экскурсии?

On what day?

**F kakóy dyén?**

В какой день?

Who is taking names for it?

**U kavóh mózhna zapissátsya?**

У кого можно записаться?

How much does it cost?

**Skólka stóyit?**

Сколько стоит?

Can one choose one's seat?

**Mózhna víbrat myésta?**

Можно выбрать место?

I'd like a front seat by the
window

**Yá khatél bi myésta fpirideé
u aknáh**

Я хотел бы место впереди
у окна

There are only centre (rear) seats
left, next to the gangway

**Astális mistáh tólka pasirideénye
(pazadeé) u prakhóda**

Остались места только посере-
дине (позади) у прохода

What time does the excursion
start?

**F katóram chassú atpravlyáyitsya
ekskúrsya?**

В котором часу отправляется
экскурсия?

| | |
|---|---|
| Where do I pick it up? | **Kudá mnyé pritée?**<br>Куда́ мне прийти́? |
| Where is the party guide? | **Gdyé rukavadéetil ekskúrsiy?**<br>Где руководи́тель экску́рсии? |
| He hasn't arrived yet | **On yishchóh ni prishól**<br>Он ещё пришёл |
| There's the interpreter. Ask him | **Vot pirivódchik. Sprasséetye yivóh**<br>Вот перево́дчик. Спроси́те его́ |
| When does the party start back? | **Kagdá grúppa atpravlyáyitsya nazát?**<br>Когда́ гру́ппа отправля́ется наза́д? |
| I'd like to walk round the park (museum) on my own | **Ya khachú pakhadéet pa párku (pa muzyéyu) adéen**<br>Я хочу́ походи́ть по па́рку (по музе́ю) оди́н |
| Mind you aren't late! | **Smatréetye, ni apazdáytye!**<br>Смотри́те не опозда́йте! |

## Amusements

| | |
|---|---|
| Are there any sporting contests on now? | **Yest tipyér kakéeye nibut spartéevniye sarivnaványa?**<br>Есть тепе́рь каки́е-нибудь спорти́вные соревнова́ния? |
| What could I watch? | **Shto yá mog bi pasmatryét?**<br>Что я мог бы посмотре́ть? |
| Where can one bathe in the river? | **Gdyé mózhna kupátsya f rikyéh?**<br>Где мо́жно купа́ться в реке́? |
| There are open-air swimming pools | **Yést atkrítiye basséyny dlyá plávanya**<br>Есть откры́тые бассе́йны для пла́вания |
| Are there any beaches? | **Yést gdyé-nibut plyázhy?**<br>Есть где́-нибудь пля́жи? |

Can you swim?

**Vi uméyitye plávat?**

Вы уме́ете пла́вать?

If you like rowing, you can hire
a boat there

**Yésly vi lyúbitye gryéblyu vi
mózhitye nanyát tam lódku**

Éсли вы лю́бите гре́блю, вы
мо́жете наня́ть там ло́дку

## Museum, gallery, exhibition

| Museums: | **Muzyéyee:** | Музе́и: |
|---|---|---|
| Anti-religious | **Antireligyózny** | Антирелигио́з-ный |
| Ethnographic | **Etnagraféechisky** | Этнографи́-ческий |
| Museum of Fine Arts | **Muzyéy izyáshnikh iskússtf** | Музе́й изя́щных иску́сств |
| Polytechnic | **Polytikhnéechisky** | Политехни́-ческий |
| Theatre | **Tiatrálny** | Театра́льный |
| Art and History of Culture (the Hermitage) | **Khudózhistvinny istórika-kultúrny (Ermitázh)** | Худо́жественный исто́рико-культу́рный (Эрмита́ж) |
| Art | **Iskússtfa** | Иску́сство |
| Department | **Atdyél** | Отде́л |
| Exhibits | **Ekspanáty** | Экспона́ты |
| Collection | **Kallyéktsya (sabránye)** | Колле́кция (собра́ние) |
| Sculpture | **Skulptúra** | Скульпту́ра |
| Sculptor | **Skúlptar** | Ску́льптор |
| Painting | **Zhéevapeess** | Жи́вопись |
| Picture | **Kartéena** | Карти́на |
| Portrait | **Partryét** | Портре́т |
| Artist | **Khudózhnik** | Худо́жник |
| Ikon-painting | **Ikónapeess** | Ико́нопись |
| Archaeology | **Arkhiaológiya** | Археоло́гия |

| | | |
|---|---|---|
| Numismatics | **Numismátika** | Нумизма́тика |
| Applied art | **Prikladnóye iskússtfa** | Прикладно́е иску́сство |
| China and Faience | **Farfór ee fayáns** | Фарфо́р и фая́нс |
| Articles made of glass (of stone, of gold, of silver) | **Izdyéliya eez stikláh (kámnya, zólata, siribrá)** | Изде́лия из стекла́ (ка́мня, зо́лота, серебра́) |
| Folk art | **Naródnaye iskússtfa** | Наро́дное иску́сство |
| Weaving | **Tkány** | Тка́ни |
| Embroidery | **Víshivky** | Вы́шивки |
| Ceramic and Wooden Toys | **Kiraméecheskiye ee dirivyánniye igrúshky** | Керами́ческие и деревя́нные игру́шки |
| Art gallery | **Kartéenaya galliryéya** | Карти́нная галере́я |
| Exhibition: | **Vístavka:** | Вы́ставка: |
| Agricultural | **Silskakhazyáy-stvinnaya** | Сельскохозя́й-ственная |
| Industrial | **Pramwíshlinnaya** | Промы́шленная |
| Constructional | **Strayéetilnaya** | Строи́тельная |
| Pavilion | **Pavilyón** | Павильо́н |

On what floor is the Ikon Dept. (Dept. of Folk Art)?

**Na kakóm etazhéh atdyél ikónapeesy (naródnava iskússtfa)?**

На како́м этаже́ отде́л иконо-писи (наро́дного иску́сства)?

Where is the collection of Toys (the Archaeological exhibits)?

**Gdyé kallyékstiy igrúshik (ekspanáty arkhialógiy)?**

Где колле́кции игру́шек (экспона́ты археоло́гии)?

Where is the Room of Twentieth Century Russian Artists?

**Gdyé zal rússkikh khudózhnikaf dvatsátava vyéka?**

Где зал ру́сских худо́жников двадца́того ве́ка?

Who was the painter of this portrait?

**Kto áftar étava partryéta?**

Кто áвтор э́того портрéта?

Who painted this picture?

**Kto napissál étu kartéenu?**

Кто написáл э́ту карти́ну?

What period does it belong to?

**Kakóva onáh vryéminy?**

Какóго онá врéмени?

Is this contemporary sculpture?

**Éta savrimyénnaya skulptúra?**

Э́то совремéнная скульптýра?

What is the name of the sculptor?

**Kak éemya skúlptara?**

Как и́мя скýльптора?

Are there any examples of classical sculpture here?

**Yést zdyés praizvidyénya antéechnay skulptúry?**

Есть здесь произведéния анти́чной скульптýры?

Where is the department of Western European Painting?

**Gdyé atdyél západna-yivrapyéy-skay zhéevopissy?**

Где отдéл зáпадно-европéй-ской жи́вописи?

Are there any pictures by English painters here?

**Yést zdyés kartéeny angléeskikh khudózhnikaf?**

Есть здесь карти́ны англи́йских худóжников?

Where is the collection of pictures of the French (Dutch, Flemish, Italian) School?

**Gdyé sabránye kartéen frantsúzkay (gallándskay, flamándskay, italyánskay) zhéevopissy?**

Где собрáние карти́н францýзской (голлáндской, фламáндской, итальáнской) жи́вописи?

On what days is this museum open?

**Pa kakéem dnyám atkrít état muzyéy?**

По каки́м дням откры́т э́тот музéй?

What time does the Exhibition close?

**Do kakóva chassá atkríta vístavka?**

До какóго чáса откры́та вы́ставка?

| | |
|---|---|
| What does it cost to go in? | **Kakáya pláta za fkhót?** |
| | Кака́я пла́та за вход? |
| May I have a guide who speaks English? | **Magú yá imyét géeda, katóry gavaréet p-angleésky?** |
| | Могу́ я име́ть ги́да, кото́рый говори́т по-англи́йски? |
| Where can I buy a catalogue (plan) of the museum? | **Gdyé mózhna kupéet katalóg (plan) muzyéya?** |
| | Где мо́жно купи́ть катало́г (план) музе́я? |
| Where do they sell picture postcards (booklets) of the museum? | **Gdyé pradayút atkrítky (albóm) muzyéya?** |
| | Где продаю́т откры́тки (альбо́м) музе́я? |
| Have you a card (photograph) of the picture . . .? | **Yést u vass atkrítka (fatagráfiya) kartéeny?** |
| | Есть у вас откры́тка (фото-гра́фия) карти́ны . . .? |
| I can't find the way out | **Yá ni magú naytée gdyé víkhat** |
| | Я не могу́ найти́ где вы́ход |
| I have lost my cloak-room ticket | **Yá patiryál nomirók at gardiróba** |
| | Я потеря́л номеро́к от гардеро́ба |
| I had a coat and an umbrella | **U minyá bwíla paltóh ee zóntik** |
| | У меня́ бы́ло пальто́ и зо́нтик |

## Church (Cathedral)

| | |
|---|---|
| What is the name of this church (cathedral)? | **Kak nazivávitsya èta tsérkaf (ètat sabór)?** |
| | Как называ́ется э́та це́рковь (э́тот собо́р)? |
| Is it an old church? | **Éta staréennaya tsérkaf?** |
| | Это стари́нная це́рковь? |
| When was it built? | **Kagdá anáh pastróyina?** |
| | Когда́ она́ постро́ена? |

| | |
|---|---|
| In the seventeenth century | **V simnátsatam vyékye**<br>В семна́дцатом ве́ке |
| Was it built by a Russian? | **Rússky arkhityéktar stróyil yiyóh?**<br>Ру́сский архите́ктор стро́ил её? |
| May I go in and look at the inside? | **Mózhna vaytée, pasmatryét yiyóh vnutrée?**<br>Мо́жно войти́, посмотре́ть её внутри́? |
| It is closed at the moment | **Sicháss onáh zapirtáh**<br>Сейча́с она́ заперта́ |
| There's a service going on now | **Sicháss idyót slúzba**<br>Сейча́с идёт слу́жба |
| You can't look round, but you can go in and stand by the entrance | **Asmátrivat nilzyá, a vaytée ee pastayát u fkhóda mózhna**<br>Осма́тривать нельзя́, а войти́ и постоя́ть у вхо́да мо́жно |
| Are there any ancient ikons here? | **Yést zdyés staréenniye ikóny?**<br>Есть здесь стари́нные ико́ны? |
| What century do they belong to? | **Kakóva anée vyéka?**<br>Како́го они́ ве́ка? |
| Is the name of the artist known? | **Izvyéstna éemya khudózhnika?**<br>Изве́стно и́мя худо́жника? |
| May I (we) talk to the priest? | **Magú yá (mózhim mi) pagavaréet sa svishchénnikam?**<br>Могу́ я (мо́жем мы) погово-ри́ть со свяще́нником? |
| Are there services every day? | **Kázhdy dyén biváyut slúzby?**<br>Ка́ждый день быва́ют слу́жбы? |
| At what time does the morning (evening) service begin? | **V katóram chassú nachináyitsya útrinnyaya (vichérnyaya) slúzba?**<br>В кото́ром часу́ начина́ется у́тренняя (вече́рняя) слу́жба? |

What cathedral do you advise us (me) to visit?

**Kakóy sabór savyétuyitye nam (mnyé) pasmatryét?**

Какóй собóр вы совéтуете нам (мне) посмотрéть?

The Uspensky and Blago-veshchensky cathedrals in the Kremlin

**Uspyénsky sabór ee Blaga-vyéshchinsky sabór f Krimlyéh**

Успéнский собóр и Благо-вéщенский собóр в Кремлé

They are interesting for their architecture, frescoes and ikons

**Anée intiryésny pa svayéy arkhityektúrye, fryéskam ee ikónam**

Они́ интерéсны по своéй архитектýре, фрéскам и икóнам

Are there services there?

**Biváyut tam bagasluzhénya?**

Быва́ют там богослужéния?

No, they are preserved and restored now only as monu-ments of ancient Russian art

**Nyét, tipyér eekh sakhranyáyut ee ristavréeruyut tólka kak pámyatniky dryévna-rússkava iskússtfa**

Нет, тепéрь их сохраня́ют и реставри́руют тóлько как па́мятники древнерýсского искýсства

Where would I be able to hear the sound of Russian bells and Russian church singing?

**Gdyé mózhna bwíla bi uslíshat rússky kalakólny svón ee rússkaye tsirkóvnaye pyénye?**

Где мóжно бы́ло бы услы́шать рýсский колокóльный звон и рýсское церкóвное пéние?

Go to the Troitse-Sergieva Monastery

**Payezháytye f Tróyitsi-Syérgyevu Lávru**

Поезжа́йте в Трóице-Сéргиеву Ла́вру

# Eating and Drinking

The Soviet Union is not a gastronomic paradise, and most meals will probably be taken in the hotel, but all visitors should try the excellent icecream, chocolate, bread and the dairy products.

There are many varieties of bread and the black 'Baradínsky Khlyép' is especially tasty. In Moscow this, and other typical breads and cakes (e.g. the small cheese cakes 'vatrúshky'), are on sale in the baker's opposite the Intourist Hotel in Gorky Street.

Dairy products are varied: 'ryázhinka', 'smitána', 'kifféer', 'tvarók' and a slightly sweetened cream cheese 'sirók' are all very good.

These foods may be on sale in the hotel 'buffyét' or can be served at breakfast with pancakes (blínchiky) and/or other small cakes.

The main meal of the day is eaten between midday and three o'clock so that it is sometimes difficult to have soup, for example, at an evening meal.

There are a few cafés where one can get a drink and a snack without queueing (the exceptions being the large hotels where such services are available) but, in the summer months, the thirsty toutist can buy a 'kvass' from a tank, or mineral water ('gazirófka') from a vending machine in the street.

One never wears outdoor clothing in a café or restaurant: coats, hats, etc., must be left in the cloakroom.

The commonest meat dishes in a restaurant will be:

| | | | |
|---|---|---|---|
| shashlýk | kebabs | shnítsil | schnitzel |
| antrikót | steak | sasséesky | frankfurters |
| langyét | steak (small) | bifshtéks | beefsteak |

There will also be 'tsiplyónak tabaká' (a chicken cut open, pressed flat, roasted and served with a garlic sauce). The visitor should try the soup 'Salyánka' that is almost a meal in itself.

Tea is never served with milk, and lemons are a rare luxury which may be available in the Intourist cafés. Coffee is usually Turkish; although 'instant' coffee may also be served; again without milk.

Alcohol should be bought in the 'Berioska' hard currency shops. They offer a comparatively cheap and wide range. Vodka is good value, and so is Georgian brandy.

## In the restaurant

| Plate | Taryélka | Таре́лка |
|---|---|---|
| Knife | Nosh | Нож |
| Fork | Véelka | Ви́лка |
| Spoon (table, dessert, tea) | Lóshka (stalóvaya, dissyértnaya, cháynaya) | Ло́жка (столо́вая, десе́ртная, ча́йная) |
| Table napkin | Salfyétka | Салфе́тка |
| Cup and saucer | Cháshka ee blyúdichka | Ча́шка и блю́дечко |
| Tumbler | Stakán | Стака́н |
| Tea-pot; kettle | Cháynik | Ча́йник |
| Coffee-pot | Kaféynik | Кофе́йник |
| Milk jug | Malóchnik | Моло́чник |
| Sugar basin | Sákharnitsa | Са́харница |
| Tray | Padnóss | Подно́с |
| Breakfast | Pyérvy záftrak | Пе́рвый за́втрак |
| Lunch | Ftaróy záftrak | Второ́й за́втрак |
| Dinner | Abyét | Обе́д |
| Supper | Úzhin | У́жин |
| Menu | Minyú | Меню́ |
| Wine list | Kárta véen | Ка́рта вин |
| Course | Blyúda | Блю́до |

| Dish | Blyúda (kúshanye) | Блю́до (ку́шанье) |
|---|---|---|
| Cold (hot) dish | Khalódnaye (garyá-cheye) blyúda | Холо́дное (горя́чее) блю́до |
| Vegetarian dish | Vigitaryánskaye blyúda | Вегетариа́нское блю́до |
| Meat (fish) dish | Myisnóye (ríbnaye) blyúda | Мясно́е (ры́бное) блю́до |
| Salt | Sol | Соль |
| Pepper | Pyérits | Пе́рец |
| Mustard | Garchéetsa | Горчи́ца |
| Oil | Mássla | Ма́сло |
| Vinegar | Úksuss | У́ксус |
| Salad cream | Mayonéss | Майоне́з |
| Tomato sauce | Tamátny sóuss | Тома́тный со́ус |
| Horse radish | Khryén | Хрен |
| Bread | Khlyép | Хлеб |
| Bread-roll } Bun } | Búlachka | Бу́лочка |
| Toast | Padzhárinny khlyép | Поджа́ренный хлеб |
| Sandwich | Buterbrót | Бутербро́д |
| Butter | Mássla | Ма́сло |
| Porridge (of oats) | Avsyánaya kásha | Овся́ная ка́ша |
| Ham | Vitchinán | Ветчина́ |
| Sausage (large continental) | Kalbasság | Колбаса́ |
| Sausages (small English type) | Sasséesky | Соси́ски |
| Egg | Yiytsón | Яйцо́ |
| Soft-boiled eggs | Yáytsa vsmyátku | Я́йца всмя́тку |
| Hard-boiled eggs | Krutéeye yáytsa | Круты́е я́йца |
| Fried eggs | Yiéeshnitsa | Яи́чница |
| Hors d'oeuvre; savoury | Zakúsky | Заку́ска |
| Thick soup, made of . . . | Sup eez . . . | Суп из . . . |
| Clear soup | Bulyón | Булья́н |
| Cabbage soup | Shchée | Щи |

| Beetroot soup | **Borshch** | Борщ |
| Fish | **Ríba** | Рыба |
| Vegetables | **Óvoshchy** | Óвощи |
| Potatoes | **Kartófil** | Картóфель |
| Salad, made of . . . | **Salát eez . . .** | Салáт из . . . |
| Sweet | **Sládkaye** | Слáдкое |
| Dessert | **Dissyért** | Десéрт |
| Ice-cream | **Marózhinaye** | Морóженое |
| Fruit | **Frúkty** | Фрýкты |
| Stewed fruit | **Kampót** | Компóт |
| Cheese | **Síyr** | Сыр |
| Beverage, drink | **Napéetak (napéetky)** | Напúток (напúтки) |
| Alcoholic drink | **Spirtnóy napéetak** | Спиртнóй напúток |
| Wine | **Vinóh** | Винó |
| Beer | **Péeva** | Пúво |
| Vodka | **Vódka** | Вóдка |
| Kvas (of grain or fruit) – national drink | **Kvass (khlyébny, fruktóvy)** | Квас (хлéбный, фруктóвый) |
| Brandy | **Kanyák** | Коньяк |
| Liqueur | **Likyór** | Ликёр |
| Mineral water | **Minirálnaya vadáh** | Минерáльная водá |
| Lemonade (made of fresh lemons) | **Limanád (eez svyézhikh limoná)** | Лимонáд (из свéжих лимóнов) |
| Fruit juice | **Fruktóvy sok** | Фруктóвый сок |
| Coffee | **Kófye** | Кóфе |
| Tea | **Cháy** | Чай |
| Milk | **Malakóh** | Молокó |
| Cream | **Sléevky** | Слúвки |
| Cocoa | **Kakáoh** | Какáо |
| Cake | **Pirózhnaye** | Пирóжное |
| Biscuits | **Pichénye** | Печéнье |
| Jam | **Varyénye** | Варéнье |
| Marmalade | **Apilséenaye varyénye** | Апельсúнное варéнье |

*Note.* Information about other foods can be found in the sections on *Shopping* and *Fishing*.

| | |
|---|---|
| Come and have dinner with me (with us) | **Paydyómtye sa mnóy (s námy) pa-abyédat** |
| | Пойдёмте со мной (с нáми) пообéдать |
| Thank you. With pleasure | **Spasséeba, s udavólstvyem** |
| | Спасúбо, с удовóльствием |
| Where is there an empty table? | **Gdyé yést svabódny stol?** |
| | Где есть свобóдный стол? |
| A table for 2, 3, 4 | **Stol na dvukh, tryókh, chitiryókh chilavyék** |
| | Стол на 2, 3, 4 человéка |
| Near the window | **Ókala aknáh** |
| | Óколо окнá |
| It will be draughty here | **Zdyés búdyit skvazéet (skvaznyák)** |
| | Здесь бýдет сквозúть (сквознáк) |
| Can we sit here? | **Mózhna syést zdyés?** |
| | Мóжно сесть здесь? |
| This table is reserved | **État stol zakázan (zányit)** |
| | Этот стол закáзан (зáнят) |
| Over here, please | **Syudá, pazhálusta** |
| | Сюдá, пожáлуйста |
| Give me the menu and the wine list | **Dáytye minyú ee kártu veen** |
| | Дáйте меню и кáрту вин |
| *Hors d'oeuvre* (*Zakússky*; Закýска) | |
| Lobster mayonnaise | **Mayanéss eez amáraf** |
| | Майонéз из омáров |
| Sardines and salad | **Sardéeny s salátam** |
| | Сардúны с салáтом |
| Caviare (black, red) | **Ikráh (chórnaya, krásnaya)** |
| | Икрá (чёрная, крáсная) |
| *Soup* (*Sup*; Суп) | |
| Tomato soup | **Sup eez pamidóraf** |
| | Суп из помидóров |
| Clear soup | **Bulyón** |
| | Бульóн |

*Fish (Ríba;* Рыба)

Steamed salmon

**Atvarnáya lassasséena**
Отварная лососина

Fried sturgeon

**Zhárinaya assitréena**
Жáреная осетрина

*Meat dishes (Myisnéeye blyudáh;* Мясные блюдá)

Chicken with rice and mush-
rooms

**Tsiplyónak s réessam ee gribámu**
Цыплёнок с рисом и грибáми

Roast lamb and french beans

**Zhárinaya baránina c fassólyu**
Жáреная барáнина с фасóлью

*Sweet (Sládkaye;* Слáдкое)

*Ices (Marózhinaye;* Морóженое)

Wild-strawberry ice

**Zimlyanéechnaye marózhinaye**
Земляничное морóженое

*Cheese (Síyr;* Сыр)

Swiss Gruyère

**Shveytsársky**
Швейцáрский

Dutch

**Gallándsky**
Голлáндский

This is a three-course dinner:
soup, roast and sweet

**Éta abyét eez tryókh blyút: sup,
zhárkaye ee sládkaye**
Это обéд из трёх блюд – суп,
жаркóе и слáдкое

I don't want all the courses (the
soup, the sweet)

**Yá ni khachú vsyékh blyút (súpa,
sládkava)**
Я не хочý всех блюд (сýпа,
слáдкого)

Can we dine à la carte?

**Mózhna yést partsyónna?**
Мóжно есть порциóнно?

What vegetarian dishes are
there?

**Kakéeye yést vigitaryánskiye
kúshanya?**
Какие есть вегетариáнские
кýшанья?

| | |
|---|---|
| What is this dish (soup) made of? | **Eez chivóh éta blyúda (état sup)?**<br>Из чегó э́то блю́до (э́тот суп)? |
| What do you recommend today? | **Shto vi rikamindúyitye sivódnya?**<br>Что вы рекоменду́ете сегóдня? |
| I can recommend the fish: cod, trout | **Magú rikamindovát ríbu: triskú, faryél**<br>Могу́ рекомендова́ть ры́бу: треску́, форе́ль |
| Today's special dish is fish with white sauce | **Dizhúrnaye blyúda – ríba pad byélim sóussam**<br>Дежу́рное блю́до – ры́ба под бе́лым сóусом |
| What roasts have you? | **Shto u vass yést na zhárkaye?**<br>Что у вас есть на жаркóе? |
| Whatever you wish: pork, roast beef, lamb, veal | **Shto vam ugódna: svinéena, róstbif, baránina, tilyátina**<br>Что вам угóдно: свини́на, рóстбиф, бара́нина, теля́тина |
| As for poultry, there is turkey, goose and duck | **Eez ptéetsy yést indéyka, guss ee útka**<br>Из пти́цы есть инде́йка, гусь и у́тка |
| A great variety of vegetables: spinach, cabbage, everything that is in season | **Mnóga ráznikh avashchéy: shpinát, kapústa, vsyóh shto pa sizóny**<br>Мнóго ра́зных овоще́й: шпина́т, капу́ста, всё что по сезóну |
| What would you like? | **Shto vam ugódna?**<br>Что вам угóдно? |
| Give me lamb chops with peas and carrots | **Dáytye mnyé atbivnéeye katlyéty s garóshkam ee markóvyu**<br>Да́йте мне отбивны́е котле́ты с горóшком и моркóвью |

Could I have kidneys, or liver
  and onion, with cauliflower?

**Magú yá paluchéet póchky éely
pichyónku s lúkam ee tsvitnóy
kapústay?**
Могу́ я получи́ть по́чки и́ли
печёнку с лу́ком и цветно́й
капу́стой?

What have you chosen?

**Shto vi víbraly?**
Что вы вы́брали?

What would you like after that?

**Shto vam yishchóh ugódna?**
Что вам ещё уго́дно?

What sort of sweet is there?

**Kakóye yést sládkaye?**
Како́е есть сла́дкое?

You can have ice-cream, or
  chocolate pudding or apple
  tart

**Mózhitye paluchéet marózhinaye,
éely shakaládny púding, éely
yáblachny pirók**
Мо́жете получи́ть моро́женое,
и́ли шокола́дный пу́динг,
и́ли я́блочный пиро́г

The strawberries and whipped
  cream are finished

**Klubnéeky sa sbéetimy sléevkamy
bólshye nyét**
Клубни́ки со сби́тыми
сли́вками бо́льше нет

Bring me some more bread
  (some butter, some water)

**Dáytye yishchóh khlyéba
(mássla, vadíy)**
Да́йте ещё хле́ба (ма́сла,
воды́)

Take this away. I didn't order
  this

**Vozméetye éta. Yá étava ni
zakázival**
Возьми́те э́то. Я э́того не
зака́зывал

This plate is not clean

**Éta taryélka ni chéestaya**
Э́та таре́лка не чи́стая

This is very nice

**Éta óchin fkússna**
Э́то о́чень вку́сно

| | |
|---|---|
| This is too sweet (sour) | **Éta sléeshkam sládka (kéesla)**<br>Это слишком сладко (кисло) |
| The meat is tough (underdone, overdone) | **Myássa zhóstkaye (nidazhárina, pirizhárina)**<br>Мясо жёсткое (недожа́рено, пережа́рено) |
| The soup is too salty | **Sup pirisólyin**<br>Суп пересо́лен |
| The fish is not fresh | **Ríba ni svyézhaya**<br>Ры́ба не свежая |
| A glass of dark ale, please | **Stakán chórnava péeva, pazhálusta**<br>Стака́н чёрного пи́ва, пожа́-луйста |
| A small glass of light (ale) | **Nibolshóy stakán svyétlava péeva**<br>Небольшо́й стака́н све́тлого пи́ва |
| This is a light table wine | **Éta lyókhaye stalóvaye vinóh**<br>Э́то лёгкое столо́вое вино́ |
| It is not iced | **Anóh ni sa ldáh**<br>Оно́ не со льда́ |
| What cold drinks have you got? | **Kakéeye yést u vass khalódniye napéetky?**<br>Каки́е есть у вас холодные напи́тки? |
| This Russian drink is not an alcoholic one, is it? | **État rússky napéetak ni spirtnóy?**<br>Э́тот ру́сский напи́ток не спиртно́й? |
| Give me a bottle of soda water (a half-bottle of lemonade) | **Dáytye butílku sódavay vadíy (polbutílky limanádu)**<br>Да́йте буты́лку со́довой воды́ (полбуты́лки лимона́ду) |
| Do you like your coffee black or with cream (milk)? | **Vi khatéetye chórny kófye éely sa sléevkamy (s malakóm)?**<br>Вы хоти́те чёрный ко́фе и́ли со сли́вками (с молоко́м)? |

| | |
|---|---|
| May I have the bill? | **Dáytye shchot**<br>Дáйте счёт |
| Pay at the desk | **Zaplateétye f kássu**<br>Заплатúте в кáссу |
| No tipping | **Chaiveéye ni palagáyutsya**<br>Чаевы́е не полагáются |
| I am very thirsty | **Mnyé khóchitsya péet**<br>Мне óчень хóчется пить |
| Would you like to have tea now? | **Khateétye sicháss péet cháy?**<br>Хотúте сейчáс пить чай? |
| I'd (we'd) like to take some tea | **Yá khachý (mi khateém) víypeet cháyu**<br>Я хочý (мы хотúм) вы́пить чáю |
| The tea is too weak | **Cháy sleéshkam sláby**<br>Чай слúшком слáбый |
| We (I) like our tea very strong | **Mi lyúbim (yá lyublyú) óchin kryépky cháy**<br>Мы лю́бим (я люблю́) óчень крéпкий чай |
| Is this the hot water? | **Éta kipyatók?**<br>Это кипятóк? |
| Bring some more hot water | **Prinisseétye yishchóh kipyatkú**<br>Принесúте ещё кипяткý |
| What would you like for tea? | **Shto vam ugódna k cháyu?**<br>Что вам угóдна к чáю? |
| We have toast, buns, pastries, cake and gâteau | **U nass yést padzhárinny khlyép, búlachky, pirózhniye, keks ee tort**<br>У нас есть поджáренный хлеб, бýлочки, пирóжные, кекс и торт |
| There are sandwiches and radishes | **Yést butirbródy ee rideéska**<br>Есть бутербрóды и редúска |
| I only want bread and butter, jam, and a slice of lemon | **Yá khachú tólka khlyép s másslam ee varyénye ee kussóchik limóna**<br>Я хочý тóлько хлеб с мáслом и варéнье и кусóчек лимóна |

| | |
|---|---|
| What would you like for breakfast? | **Shto vam ugódna k záftraku?**<br>Что вам угóдно к зáвтраку? |
| Porridge, a boiled egg, or fried egg and bacon | **Avsyánuyu káshu, yiytsóh vsmyátku éely yiéeshnitsu s vitchinóy**<br>Овсянyю кáшу, яйцó всмятку и́ли яи́чницу с ветчинóй |
| If possible, some marmalade | **Yésly vazmózhna apilséenaye varyénye**<br>Éсли возмóжно, апельси́нное варéнье |

*At table*

| | |
|---|---|
| How do you like . . .? | **Kak vam nrávitsya . . .?**<br>Как вам нрáвится . . .? |
| Can I give (pour) you some more? | **Mózhna dat (naléet) vam yishchóh?**<br>Мóжно дать (нали́ть) вам ещё? |
| Have a little more | **Skúshaytye yishchóh kussóchik**<br>Скýшайте ещё кусóчек |
| No, thank you. I've eaten (drunk) enough | **Spasséeba. Yá dastátachna yél (péel)**<br>Спаси́бо. Я достáточно ел (пил) |
| Good health! | **Za váshe zdaróvye!**<br>За вáше здорóвье! |
| Please help yourself | **Biréetye, pazhálusta, sámy**<br>Бери́те, пожáлуйста, сáми |
| Choose what you like | **Vibiráytye, shto khatéetye**<br>Выбирáйте, что хоти́те |
| Please pass the jam | **Piridáytye, pazhálusta varyénye**<br>Передáйте, пожáлуйста, варéнье |
| That is very nice | **Éta óchin fkússna**<br>Это óчень вкýсно |

| | |
|---|---|
| Would you care for a cigarette? | **Khateétye papiróssu?**<br>Хотúте папиросу? |
| May I be allowed to light my pipe? | **Razrisheétye zakuréet trúbku?**<br>Разрешúте закурúть трýбку? |
| Where are my matches? | **Gdyé mayeé spéechky?**<br>Где мой спúчки? |
| Here's a lighter | **Vot zazhigálka**<br>Вот зажигáлка |
| Pass the ash-tray, please | **Piridáytye, pazhálusta, pyépilnitsu**<br>Передáйте, пожáлуйста, пéпельницу |

# At the Post Office

| Letter | **Peessmóh** | Письмо́ |
| Postcard | **Atkrítka** | Откры́тка |
| Registered letter | **Zakaznóye peesmóh** | Заказно́е письмо́ |
| Printed matter | **Pichátny matiryál (atpravlyénye bandirólyu)** | Печа́тный материа́л (отправле́ние бандеро́лью) |
| Express | **Sróchnaye atpravlyénye** | Сро́чное отправле́ние |
| Air mail | **Ávya-póchta** | А́виапо́чта |
| Telegram | **Tiligrámma** | Телегра́мма |
| Parcel | **Passílka** | Посы́лка |
| Receipt | **Kvitántsya** | Квита́нция |
| Letter-box | **Pachtóvy yáshchik** | Почто́вый я́щик |
| Post office | **Pachtóvaye atdyilyénye** | Почто́вое отделе́ние |
| Head post office | **Glávny pachtámt** | Гла́вный почта́мт |
| Address | **Ádriss** | А́дрес |
| Addressee | **Adrissát** | Адреса́т |
| Sender | **Atpravéetyil** | Отправи́тель |
| Post-office official | **Pachtóvy slúzhashchy** | Почто́вый слу́жащий |
| Postman | **Pachtalyón** | Почтальо́н |
| Postage | **Pachtóvaya apláta** | Почто́вая опла́та |
| Stamp | **Márka** | Ма́рка |
| Post-free | **Bisplátnaya atpráfka** | Беспла́тная отпра́вка |
| Wrapper (e.g. round newspaper) | **Bandiról** | Бандеро́ль |
| Poste restante | **Póchta da vastryéba-vanya** | По́чта до востре́бования |

Has the postman been? **Prikhadéel uzhéh pachtalyón?**
Приходи́л уже́ почтальо́н?

Letters are delivered three times
a day

**Peéssma raznóssyatsya tree ráza
v dyén**

Письма разносятся три раза
в день

This morning he brought two
letters and a postcard

**Sivódnya útram bwíly palúchiny
dva peessmáh ee atkrítka**

Сегодня утром были получены
два письма и открытка

Drop this letter into the nearest
box

**Apusteétye éta peessmóh v bli-
zháyshy pachtóvy yáshchik**

Опустите это письмо в ближ-
айший почтовый ящик

The next collection is at six

**Slyédushchaya víyemka peéssim
f shyést chassóf**

Следующая выемка писем
в шесть часов

There's something to pay

**S vass palagáyitsya dapláta**

С вас полагается доплата

Please forward

**Prashú pirislát**

Прошу переслать

Where is the Poste Restante?

**Gdyé vidayút peéssma da
vastryébavanya?**

Где выдают письма до
востребования?

Are there any letters (parcels)
for me?

**Nyét ly mnyé peéssim (passílky)?**

Нет ли мне писем (посылки)?

Where can I buy stamps?

**Gdyé mózhna kupeét pachtóviye
márky?**

Где можно купить почтовые
марки?

What is the postage to England
(by air mail)?

**Kakeéye márky na peessmóh
v Ángliyu (aviapóchtay)?**

Какие марки на письмо
в Англию (авиапочтой)?

Two 50-kopeck stamps

**Dvyé márky pa pyateédissyaty
kopéyek**

Две марки по пятидесяти
копеек

Where do they deal with printed
matter (registered letters,
parcels, postal orders,
telegrams)?

**Gdyé prinimáyut bandiróly
(zakaznéeye péessma, passílky,
pirivódy, tiligrámmy)?**

Где принимáют бандерóли
(заказны́е пи́сьма, посы́лки,
перевóды, телегрáммы)?

I want to send this as printed
matter

**Khachú passlát éta bandirólyu**

Хочý послáть э́то бандерóлью

Can I register this letter?

**Mózhna atprávit éta peessmóh
zakazním?**

Мóжно отпрáвить э́то письмó
заказны́м?

Do you want to send this parcel
registered?

**Khatéetye atprávit étu passílku
zakaznóy?**

Хоти́те отпрáвить э́ту посы́лку
заказнóй?

You must fill in the special form,
which travels with the parcel

**Vi dalzhée zapólnit spitsyálny
blank, katóry atpravlyáyitsya
pri passílkye**

Вы должны́ запóлнить спе-
циáльный бланк, котóрый
отправля́ется при посы́лке

Give me a form for a money
order (telegram, parcel)

**Dáytye mnyé blank dlyá dyénizh-
nava pirivóda (tiligrámmy,
passílky)**

Дáйте мне бланк для дéнеж-
ного перевóда (телегрáммы,
посы́лки)

You haven't filled it in properly

**Vi niprávilna zapólnily**

Вы непрáвильно запóлнили

Help me to fill in the form

**Pamagéetye mnyé zapólnit blank**

Помоги́те мне запóлнить
бланк

I want to send a (priority,
international) telegram

**Yá khachú atprávit (sróchnuyu,
mizhdunaródnuyu) tiligrámmu**

Я хочý отпрáвить (срóчную,
междунарóдную) теле-
грáмму

How much per word does an
ordinary (priority) telegram
cost?

**Skólka stóyit slóva abiknavyén-
nay (sróchnay) tiligrámmy?**

Ско́лько сто́ит сло́во обыкно-
ве́нной (сро́чной) теле-
гра́ммы?

What is the rate for telegrams
to England?

**Kakóy taréef dlyá tiligrám
v Ánglyu?**

Како́й тари́ф для телегра́мм
в А́нглию?

A reply-paid telegram

**Tiligrámma s apláchinim
atvyétam**

Телегра́мма с опла́ченным
отве́том

Don't forget to put the name and
address of the sender

**Ni zabúdtye napissát eemya ee
ádriss atpraveétilya**

Не забу́дьте написа́ть и́мя и
а́дрес отправи́теля

When will it be delivered?

**Kagdá anáh búdyit dastávlina?**

Когда́ она́ бу́дет доста́влена?

Will you give me a receipt?

**Vi dadeétye mnyé kvitántsyu?**

Вы дади́те мне квита́нцию?

# Using the Telephone

|  |  |  |
|---|---|---|
| Telephone | Tilifón | Телефо́н |
| Call-box | Tilifón-aftamát | Телефо́н-автома́т |
| Receiver | (Tilifónnaya) trúbka | Телефо́нная тру́бка |
| Exchange | Stántsya | Ста́нция |
| Automatic exchange | Aftamateéchiskaya tilifónnaya stántsya (Ah Teh Ess) | Автомати́ческая телефо́нная ста́нция (атс) |
| Extension | Dabávachny Tilifón | Доба́вочный телефо́н |
| Operator | Tilifaneést(ka) | Телефони́ст(ка) |
| Subscriber | Abanyént | Абоне́нт |
| Directory | Tilifónnaya knéega | Телефо́нная кни́га |
| Call | Vízaf | Вы́зов |
| Caller | Viziváyushchy | Вызыва́ющий |
| Night call | Nachnóy vízaf | Ночно́й вы́зов |
| Local call | Garadskóy vízaf | Городско́й вы́зов |
| Trunk call (long distance) | Inagaródny vízaf | Иногоро́дний вы́зов |
| Connection | Svyáz | Связь |
| Engaged | Zányita | За́нято |
| To connect | Sayedinyát (Sayedinéet) | Соединя́ть (*perf.* соедини́ть) |
| To dial | Nabirát (Nabrát) | Набира́ть (*perf.* набра́ть) |
| To ring up (to call on the phone) | Pazvanéet pa tilifónu (vizivát, *perf.* vízvat pa tilifónu) | Позвони́ть по телефо́ну (вызыва́ть, *perf.* вы́звать по телефо́ну) |

**Are you on the phone?** — **U vass yést tilifón?**
У вас есть телефо́н?

We can make an appointment by telephone

**Mi mózhim sgavareétsya o vstryéche pa tilifóny**

Мы мóжем сговори́ться о встрéче по телефóну

I'll give you an answer by phone

**Yá dam vam atvyét pa tilifónu**

Я дам вам отвéт по телефóну

Ring me up tomorrow evening

**Pazvaneétye mnyé záftra vyéchiram**

Позвони́те мне зáвтра вéчером

Hullo! Is that number 5642?

**Allyóh! Éta nómir pyatdissyát shest – sórak dva?**

Аллó! Это нóмер пятьдеся́т шесть – сóрок два? (56-42)

Sorry! Wrong number

**Prasteétye, éta asheépka**

Прости́те, это оши́бка

Who is that speaking?

**Kto gavareét?**

Кто говори́т?

This is X speaking

**(S vámy) gavareét X**

(С вáми) говори́т X

Speak more clearly (louder)

**Gavareétye yasnyéyeh (grómche)**

Говори́те яснéе (грóмче)

I can't hear you very well

**Yá plókha vass slíshu**

Я плóхо вас слы́шу

Can I speak to X?

**Magú yá pagavareét s X?**

Могу́ я поговори́ть с X?

Ask X to come to the phone

**Paprasseétye k tilifóny X**

Попроси́те к телефóну X

Hullo! We were cut off

**Allyóh! Nass razyidineély**

Аллó! Нас разъедини́ли

Tell him (her) that K rang

**Piridáytye yimú (yéy) shto svaneél(a) K**

Передáйте ему́ (ей), что звони́л(а) K

You are wanted on the phone

**Vass prósyat k tilifóny**

Вас прóсят к телефóну

Ask X to ring me

**Paprasseétye X pazvaneét mnyé**

Попроси́те X позвони́ть мне

Make a note of my number

**Zapishe\'etye móy nómir**

Запиши́те мой но́мер

Hold the line! Don't replace the receiver!

**Padazhde\'etye! Ni kladee\'tye trúpku**

Подожди́те! Не клади́те тру́бку

I'll ring later

**Ya pazvanyú pózhe**

Я позвоню́ по́зже

Can I telephone from here?

**Mózhna pagavaree\'et atsyúda pa tilifónu?**

Мо́жно поговори́ть отсю́да по телефо́ну?

Is your telephone automatic?

**U vass tilifón-aftamát?**

У вас телефо́н-автома́т?

How do I dial?

**Kak náda nabirát?**

Как на́до набира́ть?

Lift the receiver

**Snimee\'tye trúpku**

Сними́те тру́бку

Then dial the required number

**Zatyém nabiráytye nómir**

Зате́м набира́йте тре́буемый но́мер

Help me to call number . . .

**Pamagee\'etye mnyé vízvat nómir . . .**

Помоги́те мне вы́звать но́мер . . .

Is that the exchange?

**Éta tsintrálnaya?**

Э́то центра́льная?

Give me number 5036

**Dáytye pyatdissyát – tree\'etsat shest**

Да́йте пятьдеся́т – три́дцать шесть (50-36)

You're through!

**Sayedinee\'ela. Gavaree\'etye!**

Соедини́ла. Говори́те!

Engaged

**Zányita**

За́нято

There's no answer

**Ni atvicháyut**

Не отвеча́ют

| | |
|---|---|
| Replace the receiver and repeat the call | **Pavyésstye trúpku ee vizivaýtye snóva** |
| | Повéсьте трýбку и вызывáйте снóва |
| Insert the coin when the exchange tells you | **Apustéetye manyétu, kagdá vam skázhit stántsya** |
| | Опустúте монéту, когдá вам скáжет стáнция |
| I can't get through | **Ni magú sayedinéet** |
| | Не могý соединúть |
| The telephone is out of order | **Tilifón ispórchin** |
| | Телефóн испóрчен |
| Give me Enquiries | **Dáytye správachnuyu** |
| | Дáйте спрáвочную |
| Give me Trunks (International) | **Dáytye inagaródnuyu (mizhdu-naródnuyu)** |
| | Дáйте иногорóднюю (между-нарóдную) |
| Is that the Travel Bureau? | **Éta byuróh putishéstviy?** |
| | Это бюрó путешéствий? |
| Extension 4, please | **Dabávachny nómir chitírye, pazhálusta** |
| | Добáвочный нóмер четы́ре, пожáлуйста |
| Just a moment. Don't replace the receiver | **Adnú minútu, ni kladéetye trúpku** |
| | Однý минýту, не кладúте трýбку |
| Give me Telegrams | **Dáytye tiligráf** |
| | Дáйте телегрáф |

# Shopping

Souvenirs, books and luxury goods are best bought at the special hard-currency shops called БЕРЁЗКА (Biryóska), where prices are lower than in ordinary shops and a wider range of goods is available. These shops may be within a hotel but, in big cities, are separate. Purchases at these shops can be made in any currency except that of Soviet or other eastern bloc countries. Foreign language newspapers are sometimes available if they do not carry any criticism of the USSR; but there is no regular supply of any one paper.

Most visitors to the Soviet Union will want to visit the 'ordinary' shops. This is a rather complicated and time-consuming business, but there are 'short-cuts'. First, having decided what you want, make sure that there is a plentiful supply. Note the price (write it down if necessary) and go to the cash desk and pay (the shop assistant who is serving never takes money). At the cash desk, name the section you are buying from, either by name or number, (it is always clearly displayed), and the sum. Take your receipt back to the counter and give it to the assistant.

If you have to queue, wish to examine the goods you are buying in advance, or try something on, then a different procedure is used. Once you have decided on your purchase, ask the assistant to write down the amount. Pay at the cash desk and return to the counter, but do not stand in the queue or wait again. Proffer your receipt and take your purchase at once. In some stores you receive your purchase from a special counter.

Dva rublyáh shest kapyéyik, pazhálusta.
2 roubles 6 kopecks, please.

Tryéty atdyel.
Section 3.

Vóssyim rublyéy.
Eight roubles.

Rubáshky.
Shirt Department.

Vípisheetye mnyé éta, pazhálusta.
Write a bill for this please.

Yá éta vazmú.
I'd like to buy it.

When buying small items, like cakes, stamps, or icecreams, it is easy to explain what you want by saying the number of things you want and 'za' and the price in numbers only: 'Two 25 kopeck icecreams', would be: 'Dva za dvátsat pyát, pazhálusta', etc.

In some shops you have to hand in your shopping bag before entering or open it for inspection on leaving. It is also worth remembering when buying food, to take a supply of bags and carriers as all articles come unwrapped.

There may be shortages of certain products – especially toiletries (toilet rolls, sanitary towels, tissues etc); the tourist is advised to pack everything he is likely to need during his visit.

Tourist 'bargains' are similarly subject to shortages, but the following are well worth looking for: linen sheets and tablecloths; amber; fur hats and gloves; small leather goods; playing cards; semi-precious stones (e.g. from Siberia and the Urals); traditional craftware (lace, filigree etc); and stationery.

## General words and expressions

| | | |
|---|---|---|
| Store, shop, department | **Magazéen, lávka, atdyél** | Магази́н, ла́вка, отде́л |
| Department store | **Univermág (universálny magazéen)** | Универма́г (универса́льный магази́н) |

| | | |
|---|---|---|
| Bakery | **Búlachnaya** | Бу́лочная |
| Confectioner's | **Kandéetirskaya** | Конди́терская |
| Butcher's | **Myissnáya lávka** | Мясна́я ла́вка |
| Fishmonger's | **Ríbnaya lávka** | Ры́бная ла́вка |
| Greengrocer's | **Avashnáya lávka** | Овощна́я ла́вка |
| Provision merchant | **Gastranóm** | Гастроно́м |
| Dispensing chemist | **Aptyéka** | Апте́ка |
| Parfumier | **Parfyumyérya** | Парфюме́рия |
| Stationer's | **Kantstaváry** | Канцтова́ры |
| Haberdasher's | **Galantiryéyny magazéen** | Галантере́йный магази́н |
| Cleaner and Dyer | **Chéestka ee kráska** | Чи́стка и кра́ска |
| Outfitter | **Magazéen adyézhdy** | Магази́н оде́жды |
| Shoe-shop | **Magazéen óbuvy** | Магази́н о́буви |
| Handicraft shop | **Magazéen kustárnikh izdyéliy** | Магази́н куста́рных изде́лий |
| Tobacconist's (Cigarette stall) | **Tabáchnaya lávka (tabáchny kiósk)** | Таба́чная ла́вка (таба́чный кио́ск) |
| Book-shop | **Knéezhny magazéen** | Кни́жный магази́н |
| Market | **Rínak (bazár)** | Ры́нок (база́р) |
| Salesman | **Pradavyéts** | Продаве́ц |
| Customer | **Pakupátyel** | Покупа́тель |
| To buy | **Pakupát** (*perf.* **kupéet**) | Покупа́ть (*perf.* купи́ть) |
| To go shopping | **Khadéet za pakúpkamy** | Ходи́ть за поку́пками |
| To sell | **Pradavát** | Продава́ть |
| To choose, select | **Vibirát** | Выбира́ть |
| To order | **Zakazát** | Заказа́ть |
| To cancel an order | **Atminéet zakás** | Отмени́ть зака́з |
| To exchange | **Abminyát** | Обменя́ть |
| To deliver | **Dastávit** | Доста́вить |
| To take | **Vzyát** | Взять |
| To wrap up | **Zavirnút** | Заверну́ть |
| Basket | **Karzéenka** | Корзи́нка |

Is the shop open on Sunday? **Atkrít magazéen v vaskrisyénye?**
Откры́т магази́н в воскресе́нье?

| | |
|---|---|
| What time does it open (close)? | **F katóram chassú atkriváyitsya (zakriváyitsya)?**<br>В котóром часý открывáется (закрывáется)? |
| Where is the clothing (shoe) department? | **Gdyé atdyél adyézhdy (óbuvy)?**<br>Где отдéл одéжды (óбуви)? |
| What can I do for you? | **Shto magú vam pridlazhéet?**<br>Что могý вам предложúть? |
| Are you being served? | **Vámy zanimáyutsya?**<br>Вáми занимáются? |
| Have you . . .? | **Yést u vass . . .?**<br>Есть у вас . . .? |
| I need . . . | **Mnyé núzhin (nuzhnáh, núzhna, núzhny) . . .**<br>Мне нýжен (нужнá, нýжно, нýжны) . . . |
| Show me . . . | **Pakazhéetye mnyé . . .**<br>Покажúте мне . . . |
| This is not exactly what I need | **Éta ni savsyém to, shto mnyé núzhna**<br>Это не совсéм то, что мне нýжно |
| I don't like that | **Éta mnyé ni nrávitsya**<br>Это мне не нрáвится |
| Is there something better? | **Yést shto-nibút palúchshe?**<br>Есть что-нибýдь полýчше? |
| How much does this cost? | **Skólka éta stóit?**<br>Скóлько это стóит? |
| It's too dear | **Sléeshkam dóraga**<br>Слúшком дóрого |
| Is there something cheaper? | **Yést dishévlye?**<br>Есть дешéвле? |
| Is there another colour? | **Yést drugóva tsvyéta?**<br>Есть другóго цвéта? |
| Is the price the same? | **Tsináh adinákavaya (takáyazhe)?**<br>Ценá одинáковая (такáя-же)? |
| This will do | **Éta gadéetsya**<br>Это годúтся |

| | |
|---|---|
| I'll take this | **Yá vazmú éta** |
| | Я возьму́ э́то |
| I'd like to try it on | **Yá khachú primyérit** |
| | Я хочу́ приме́рить |
| It's too small | **Sléeshkam mal (maláh, malóh, malée)** |
| | Сли́шком мал (мала́, мало́, малы́) |
| It's too big for me | **Mnyé viléek (vilikáh, vilikóh, vilikée)** |
| | Мне вели́к (велика́, велико́, велики́) |
| It fits well (badly) | **Kharashóh (plókha) sidéet** |
| | Хорошо́ (пло́хо) сиди́т |
| Unfortunately it's all sold | **K sazhalyényu, vsyóh paspródana** |
| | К сожале́нию, всё распро́дано |
| Please do not touch the goods on the counter | **Prósba ni trógat vyeshchéy na prilávkye** |
| | Про́сьба не тро́гать веще́й на прила́вке |
| Do I pay you, or at the cash desk? | **Kudá platéet – vam éely f kassú?** |
| | Куда́ плати́ть – вам и́ли в ка́ссу? |
| Where does one collect the parcels? | **Gdyé vidayút pakúpky?** |
| | Где выдаю́т поку́пки? |
| Collect your purchases here! | **Vídacha pakúpak** |
| | Вы́дача покупок |
| Wrap it up well | **Zavirnéetye kharashóh** |
| | Заверни́те хороше́нько |
| I'll take this with me | **Yá vazmú éta s sabóy** |
| | Я возьму́ э́то с собо́й |
| Can you send this to me at the hotel (at this address)? | **Mózhitye prislát mnyé v gastéenitsu (pa étamu ádrissu)?** |
| | Мо́жете присла́ть мне в гости́ницу (по э́тому а́дресу)? |
| Goods delivered! | **Dastáfka ná dom** |
| | Доста́вка на́ дом |

## At the baker's

| | | |
|---|---|---|
| Bakery | **Búlachnaya** | Бу́лочная |
| A loaf (Vienna loaf) | **Khlyép (búlka)** | Хлеб (бу́лка) |
| A roll ⎫<br>A bun ⎭ | **Búlachka** | Бу́лочка |
| White | **Byély** | Бе́лый |
| Brown | **Chórny** | Чёрный |
| Rye- | **Rzhanóy** | Ржано́й |
| Cake | **Keks** | Кекс |
| Gâteau | **Tort** | Торт |
| Small pastries and cakes | **Pirózhniye** | Пиро́жные |
| New, fresh | **Svyézhiy** | Све́жий |
| Stale | **Chórstvy** | Чёрствый |

| | | |
|---|---|---|
| One white loaf and half a rye-loaf | **Adéen byély khlyép ee palavéenu rzhanóva khlyéba** | Оди́н бе́лый хлеб и полови́ну ржано́го хле́ба |
| Six rolls, four buns, some cake and a fruit gâteau | **Shest khlyépstif, chitírye búlachky, keks ee tort s frúktamy** | Шесть хле́бцев, четы́ре бу́лочки, кекс и торт с фру́ктами |

## At the confectioner's

| | | |
|---|---|---|
| Confectioner's | **Kandeétirskaya** | Конди́терская |
| Sweets with fillings (centres) | **Kanfyéty (s nachéenkay)** | Конфе́ты (с начи́нкой) |
| Boiled sweets | **Lidintsíy** | Леденцы́ |
| Chocolates | **Shakaládniye kanfyéty** | Шокола́дные конфе́ты |
| Bar of chocolate | **Pléetka shakaláda** | Пли́тка шокола́да |
| A box of sweets | **Karópka kanfyét** | Коро́бка конфе́т |

## Dairy produce

| Milk | **Malakóh** | Молоко́ |
| Cream | **Sléevky** | Сли́вки |
| Butter | **Mássla** | Ма́сло |
| | **(sléevachnaye)** | (сли́вочное) |
| Curds | **Tvarók** | Творо́г |
| Sour milk | **Practakvásha** | Простоква́ша |
| Sour cream | **Smitána** | Смета́на |
| Cheese | **Síyr** | Сыр |
| Egg (eggs) | **Yiytsóh (yáytsa)** | Яйцо́ (я́йца) |

## Provision store

| A provision shop | **Magazéen pradavól-** | Магази́н продо- |
| | **stvinnikh** | во́льственных |
| | **pradúktaf** | проду́ктов |
| Departments: | **Atdyély:** | Отде́лы: |
| Groceries | **Pradavólstvinny** | Продово́льствен- |
| | | ный |
| Cooked meat and | **Kalbássny** | Колба́сный |
| sausage | | |
| Fruit | **Fruktóvy** | Фрукто́вый |
| Vegetables | **Avashnóy** | Овощно́й |
| Meat | **Myissnóy** | Мясно́й |
| Fish | **Ríbny** | Ры́бный |
| Wine | **Véenny** | Ви́нный |
| Confectionery | **Kandéetirsky** | Конди́терский |
| General | **Óbshchiy** | О́бщий |
| Fruit: | **Frúkty:** | Фру́кты: |
| Apples | **Yáblaky** | Я́блоки |
| | **(*sing.* yáblaka)** | (*sing.* я́блоко) |
| Pears | **Grúshy** | Гру́ши |
| | **(*sing.* grúsha)** | (*sing.* гру́ша) |
| Orange(s) | **Apilséen(y)** | Апельси́н(ы) |
| Grapefruit | **Greypfrút** | Грейпфру́т |
| Grapes | **Veenagrát** | Виногра́д |

| | | |
|---|---|---|
| Plums | **Sléevy** | Сли́вы |
| | (*sing.* **sléeva**) | (*sing.* сли́ва) |
| Cherries | **Véeshny** | Ви́шни |
| | (**chiryéshnya**) | (чере́шня) |
| Melon | **Dínya** | Ды́ня |
| Water-melon | **Arbús** | Арбу́з |
| Pineapple | **Ananáss** | Анана́с |
| Peach(es) | **Pyérsik(y)** | Пе́рсик(и) |
| Apricot(s) | **Abrikóss(y)** | Абрико́с(ы) |
| Bananas | **Banány** | Бана́ны |
| Currants | **Smaródina** | Сморо́дина |
| Gooseberries | **Krizhóvnik** | Крыжо́вник |
| Raspberries | **Maléena** | Мали́на |
| Wild strawberries | **Zimlinéeka** | Земляни́ка |
| Strawberries | **Klubnéeka** | Клубни́ка |
| Lemon | **Limón** | Лимо́н |
| Nuts | **Aryékhy** | Оре́хи |
| Vegetables: | **Óvashchy:** | О́вощи: |
| Potatoes | **Kartófil** | Карто́фель |
| Carrots | **Markóf** | Морко́вь |
| Cabbage | **Kapústa** | Капу́ста |
| Cauliflower | **Tsvitnáya kapústa** | Цветна́я капуста |
| Cucumbers | **Agurtsíy** | Огурцы́ |
| Green (runner) beans | **Fassól** | Фасо́ль |
| Green peas | **Zilyóny garóshik** | Зелёный горо́шек |
| Spinach | **Shpinát** | Шпина́т |
| Lettuce | **Salát** | Сала́т |
| Radish | **Ridéeska** | Реди́ска |
| Beetroot | **Svyókla** | Свёкла |
| Mushrooms | **Gribíy** | Грибы́ |
| Onion | **Luk** | Лук |
| Tomatoes | **Pamidóry (tamáty)** | Помидо́ры |
| | | (тома́ты) |
| Meat: | **Myássa:** | Мя́со: |
| Beef | **Gavyádina** | Говя́дина |
| Veal | **Tilyátina** | Теля́тина |

| Mutton (lamb) | **Baránina** | Бара́нина |
| Pork | **Svineéna** | Свини́на |
| Kidneys | **Póchky** | По́чки |
| Liver | **Pichyónka** | Печёнка |
| Tongue | **Yazík** | Язы́к |
| Roast; fried | **Zháriny (-aya)** | Жа́реный (-ая) |
| Casseroled; braised | **Tushóny** | Тушёный |
| Boiled | **Varyóny** | Варёный |
| Steamed | **Atvarnóy** | Отварно́й |
| Baked | **Pichóny** | Печёный |
| Smoked | **Kapchóny** | Копчёный |
| Beef steak | **Bifshtyéks** | Бифште́кс |
| Roast beef | **Róstbif** | Ро́стбиф |
| Chop | **Atbivnáya katlyéta** | Отбивна́я котле́та |
| Hamburger | **Rúblinaya katlyéta** | Ру́бленая котле́та |
| Poultry: | **Ptéetsa:** | Пти́ца: |
| Chicken | **Kúritsa** | Ку́рица |
| Young chicken; broiler | **Tsiplyónak** | Цыплёнок |
| Duck | **Útka** | У́тка |
| Goose | **Gus** | Гусь |
| Turkey | **Indyéyka** | Инде́йка |
| Fish: | **Ríba:** | Ры́ба: |
| Cod | **Triskáh** | Треска́ |
| Sole | **Kámbala** | Ка́мбала |
| Halibut | **Páltus** | Па́лтус |
| Trout | **Faryél** | Форе́ль |
| Herring | **Silyótka** | Селёдка |
| Sturgeon | **Assitreéna** | Осетри́на |
| Lobster | **Amár** | Ома́р |
| Crab | **Krap** | Краб |
| Caviare | **Eekráh** | Икра́ |
| Fresh | **Svyézhy** | Све́жий |
| Salted | **Salyóny** | Солёный |

| Pickled | **Marinóvany** | Маринóваный |
| Smoked | **Kapchóny** | Копчёный |
| Fish cake | **Ríbnaya katlyéta** | Рыбная котлéта |

## At the greengrocer's

| Have you any eating apples? | **Yést u vass sládkiye yáblaky?** |
| | Есть у вас сладкие яблоки? |
| Give me one kilo of pears | **Dáytye mnyé kilóh grush** |
| | Дайте мне кило груш |
| The tomatoes and radishes are cheap and very fresh | **Pamidóry ee ridéeska dyóshivy ee savsyém svyézhiye** |
| | Помидóры и редúска дёшевы и совсéм свéжие |
| Strawberries are out of season | **Sicháss ni sizón dlyá klubnéeky** |
| | Сейчáс не сезóн для клубники |
| Have you any gooseberries or (black) currants? | **Yést u vass krizhóvnik éely smaródina?** |
| | Есть у вас крыжóвник или смородина? |
| Will you have any cherries tomorrow? | **Búdut u vass záftra véeshny?** |
| | Бýдут у вас зáвтра вишни? |

## In the department store

| We have a large selection | **U nass balshóy víbar** |
| | У нас большóй выбор |
| Does this material wash well? | **Kharashóh steeráyitsya éta matyérya?** |
| | Хорошó стирáется эта матéрия? |
| The colour does not run in the wash | **Anáh v stéerkye ni linyáyit** |
| | Онá в стúрке не линяет |
| Is this a cotton material? | **Éta (khlapcháta) bumázhnaya matyérya?** |
| | Это (хлопчáто) бумáжная матéрия? |

Is this material plastic?

**Éta matyérya eez plastmássy?**
Эта матéрия из пластмáссы?

A reel of black sewing cotton, please

**Katúshku chórnikh néetak, pazhálusta**
Катýшку чёрных нúток, пожáлуйста

Three metres of this white elastic

**Tree myétra étay byélay rizéenky**
Три мéтра этой бéлой резúнки

I also need a zip-fastener

**Mnyé tákzhe nuzhnáh zastyózhka-mólnya**
Мне тáкже нужнá застёжка-мóлния

Have you small work-boxes with scissors, thimble, tape and buttons?

**Yést u vass rabóchiye yáshchichky s nózhnitsamy, napyórstkam, tissmóy ee púgavitsamy?**
Есть у вас рабóчие ящички с нóжницами, напéрстком, тесьмóй и пýговицами?

I want a plain blue tie and a handkerchief of the same colour

**Mnyé núzhin prastóy séeniy gálstuk ee nassavóy platók tavóh-zhe tsvyéta**
Мне нýжен простóй сúний гáлстук и носовóй платóк тогó-же цвéта

## Cleaning and dyeing

I want to have my suit cleaned

**Yá khachú atdát f chéestku svóy kastyúm**
Я хочý отдáть в чúстку свой костюм

Do you do invisible mending?

**Dyélayitye ly vi nizamyétnuyu pachéenku?**
Дéлаете ли вы незамéтную почúнку?

When can I call for it?

**Kagdá magú zaytée za néem?**
Когдá могý зайтú за ним?

## At the chemist

| Medicine | Likárstva | Лека́рство |
|---|---|---|
| A cure for sickness, etc. | Sryédstva at tashnatíy | Сре́дство от тошноты́ и т. д. |
| Powders | Parashkée | Порошки́ |
| Pills | Pilyúly | Пилю́ли |
| Tablets | Tablyétky | Табле́тки |
| Ointment | Mas | Мазь |
| Mixture | Mikstúra | Микстру́ра |
| Bandage | Béent | Бинт |
| Gauze | Márlya | Ма́рля |
| Cotton-wool | Váta | Ва́та |
| Plaster (adhesive) | Plástiyr | Пла́стырь |

Can you give me something for a head-ache (a cold, sickness, stomach trouble)?

**Mózhitye dat shto-nibút at galavnóy bóly (at násmarka, at tashnatíy, at rasstróystva zhilútka)?**

Мо́жете дать что-нибу́дь от головно́й бо́ли (от на́сморка, от тошноты́, от расстро́йства желу́дка)?

A box of cough-sweets

**Karópku kanfyét at káshlya**

Коро́бку конфе́т от ка́шля

Can you recommend me a throat gargle?

**Mózhitye rikomindavát mnyé palaskánye dlyá górla?**

Мо́жете рекомендова́ть мне полоска́нье для го́рла?

A bottle of peroxide and some plaster (iodine, surgical spirit)

**Butílku pyérikissy ee plástiyr (yót, spéert)**

Буты́лку пе́рекиси и пла́стырь (и́од, спирт)

A large (small) packet of cotton-wool

**Balshóy (nibalshóy) pakyét váty**

Большо́й (небольшо́й) паке́т ва́ты

Do you keep hot-water bottles?

**Yést u vass gryélky?**

Есть у вас гре́лки?

Can you make up this
prescription?

**Prigatóftye likárstva pa étamu
ritséptu**

Приготóвьте лекáрство по
э́тому реце́пту

When will the medicine be
ready?

**Kagdá búdyit gatóva likárstva?**

Когдá бýдет готóво лекáрство?

To be taken:

**Prinimát:**

Принимáть:

– after meals

– **pósslye yedíy**

– пóсле еды́

– before meals

– **pyérid yedóy**

– пе́ред едóй

– before bedtime

– **pyérid snom**

– пе́ред сном

– every four hours

– **kázhdy chitírye chassáh**

– кáждые четы́ре чáса

– dose: ten drops

– **pa dyéssyat kápyel**

– по де́сять кáпель

– dose: one teaspoonful

– **pa cháynay lózhkye**

– по чáйной лóжке

– dose: one tablespoonful

– **pa stalóvay lózhkye**

– по столóвой лóжке

For external use

**Dlyá narúzhnava upatriblyénya**

Для нарýжного употребле́ния

Shake the bottle before taking

**Vzbaltát pyérid priyómam**

Взболтáть пе́ред приёмом

# The perfumery

| Cosmetics department | **Parfyumyérny atdyél** | Парфюме́рный отде́л |
| Perfume; scent | **Dukheé** | Духи́ |
| Powder | **Púdra** | Пýдра |
| Eau-de-Cologne | **Odikalón** | Одеколóн |
| Face-cream | **Kryém dlyá litsháh** | Крем для лицá |
| Hand-cream | **Kryém dlyá ruk** | Крем для рук |

| Lipstick | **Gubnáya pamáda** | Губна́я пома́да |
| Eyebrow pencil | **Karandásh dlyá bravyéy** | Каранда́ш для бровéй |
| Toilet soap | **Twalyétnaye mwíla** | Туалéтное мы́ло |
| Shaving cream | **Pásta dlyá brityáh** | Па́ста для бритья́ |
| Shampoo | **Shampoón** | Шампу́нь |
| Toothpaste | **Zubnáya pásta** | Зубна́я па́ста |
| Toothbrush | **Zubnáya shchótka** | Зубна́я щётка |
| Nailbrush | **Shchótka dlyá naktyéy** | Щётка для ногтéй |
| Comb | **Gribyónka** | Гребёнка |
| Safety razor | **Bizapásnaya bréetva** | Безопа́сная бри́тва |
| Razor blades | **Lyézvya dlyá bréetvy** | Лéзвия для бри́твы |

## Haberdashery

| Articles for toilet and personal use | **Pridmyéty twalyéta ee léechnava abikhóda** | Предмéты туалéта и ли́чного обихо́да |
| Thread; cotton (sewing) | **Néetky** | Ни́тки |
| Needles | **Igólky** | Иго́лки |
| Pins | **Bulávky** | Була́вки |
| Buttons | **Púgavitsy** | Пу́говицы |
| Purses | **Kashilkée** | Кошельки́ |
| Wallets; brief-cases | **Partfyély** | Портфéли |
| Straps; belts | **Rimnée** | Ремни́ |
| Suit-cases | **Chimadány** | Чемода́ны |
| Brushes | **Shchótky** | Щётки |
| Mirrors | **Zirkaláh** | Зеркала́ |
| Razors | **Bréetvy** | Бри́твы |
| Head-scarves | **Platkée** | Платки́ |
| Belts | **Payassáh** | Пояса́ |
| Stockings | **Chulkée** | Чулки́ |
| Gloves, etc. | **Pirchátky, ee drugiye** | Перча́тки и др. |

## Peasant-craft shop

| Articles for gifts | **Vyéshchy dlyá padárkaf** | Вéщи для подáрков |
|---|---|---|
| Box | **Karópka** | Корóбка |
| Cigarette-case | **Partsigár** | Портсигáр |
| Cigarette-box | **Yáshchik dlyá papiróss** | Ящик для папирóс |
| Salt-cellar | **Salónka** | Солóнка |
| Tea-caddy | **Cháynitsa** | Чáйница |
| Russian shirt | **Rússkaya rubáshka** | Рýсская рубáшка |
| Ukrainian dress | **Ukrayéenskaye plátye** | Украúнское плáтье |
| Caucasian shawl | **Kavkáskaya shal** | Кавкáзская шаль |
| Uzbek cap | **Uzbyékskaya shápka** | Узбéкская шáпка |
| Tatar slippers | **Tatárskiye túfly** | Татáрские тýфли |
| Toys | **Igrúshky** | Игрýшки |

What is this for?
**Dlyá chivóh éta?**
Для чегó это?

Where was this made?
**Gdyé éta sdyélana?**
Где это сдéлано?

What wood is it made from?
**Eez kakóva dyériva?**
Из какóго дéрева?

It's birch (oak, fir, pine)
**Eez biryózy (dúba, yély, sasníy)**
Из берёзы (дýба, éли, сосны)

What stone is it made from?
**Eez kakóva kámnya?**
Из какóго кáмня?

What material is it made of?
**Eez kakóva matiryála?**
Из какóго материáла?

It's pure silver (gold)
**Eez chéestova siribráh (zólata)**
Из чúстого серебрá (зóлота)

It's made from Siberian stone
**Eez sibéerskava kámnya**
Из сибúрского кáмня

It's made from bone
**Eez kóssty**
Из кóсти

It's made of papier-mâché
**Eez papyéh-mashéy**
Из папьé-машé

This is hand-made — **Éta ruchnáya rabóta**
Это ручна́я рабо́та

This is an antique — **Éta staréennaya vyéshch**
Это стари́нная вещь

Have you an antique department? — **Yést u vass antikvárny atdyél?**
Есть у вас антиква́рный отде́л?

## At the tobacconist

| | | |
|---|---|---|
| Russian cigarettes (card tips) | **Papiróssy** | Папиро́сы |
| English-type cigarettes | **Sigaryéty** | Сигаре́ты |
| Cigar | **Sigára** | Сига́ра |
| Pipe | **Trúpka** | Тру́бка |
| Tobacco | **Tabák** | Таба́к |
| Pipe-tobacco | **Tabák dlyá trúpky** | Таба́к для тру́бки |
| Matches | **Spéechky** | Спи́чки |
| Cigarette-lighter | **Zazhigálka** | Зажига́лка |
| Flints | **Krimnée** | Кремни́ |
| Wick | **Fitéel** | Фити́ль |
| Lighter-fuel | **Spéert** | Спирт |
| Cigarette-holder | **Mundshtúk** | Мундшту́к |
| Ash | **Pyépil** | Пе́пел |
| Ash-tray | **Pyépilnitsa** | Пе́пельница |
| To smoke | **Kuréet** | Кури́ть |

Can you recommend me a mild cigar? — **Mózhitye rikamindavát mnyé slábuyu sigáru?**
Мо́жете рекомендова́ть мне сла́бую сига́ру?

What brand of cigarette do you keep? — **Kakóy márky papiróssy u vass?**
Како́й ма́рки папиро́сы есть у вас?

Have you any lighter-flints (wick, fuel)? — **Yést u vass krimnée (fitilée, spéert) dlyá zazhigálky?**
Есть у вас кремни́ (фитили́, спирт) для зажига́лки?

| Where are my matches? | **Gdyé moyeé speéchky?** |
| | Где мой спи́чки? |

## Newspapers and books

| Newspaper | **Gazyéty** | Газе́та |
| Magazine; periodical | **Zhurnál** | Журна́л |
| Bookstall | **Kiósk** | Кио́ск |
| Newsvendor | **Gazyétchik** | Газе́тчик |
| Illustrated magazine | **Illyustriróvanny zhurnál** | Иллюстри́рован-ный журна́л |
| Monthly (weekly, yearly) periodical | **Yizhimyésichny (yizhinidyélny, yizhigódny) zhurnál** | Ежеме́сячный (еженеде́льный, ежего́дный) журна́л |
| Fashion paper | **Zhurnál mot** | Журна́л мод |
| Article | **Statyáh** | Статья́ |
| Leading article | **Piridaváya statyáh (piridaveétsa)** | Передова́я статья́ (передови́ца) |
| Dictionary | **Slavár** | Слова́рь |
| Phrase-book | **Razgavórnik** | Разгово́рник |
| English-Russian | **Ángla-rússky** | А́нгло-ру́сский |
| Russian-English | **Rússka-angleésky** | Ру́сско-англи́йский |
| Guide-book | **Putivadeétyil** | Путеводи́тель |

| Has the morning paper come? | **Palúchina útrinyaya gazyéta?** |
| | Полу́чена у́тренняя газе́та? |
| Get me an evening paper | **Dastántye mnyé vichérnyuyu gazyétu** |
| | Доста́ньте мне вече́рнюю газе́ту |
| Are these the latest magazines? | **Éty zhurnály paslyédniye?** |
| | Э́ти журна́лы после́дние? |

| | |
|---|---|
| What's the news? | **Kakéeye paslyédniye izvyéstya?**<br>Какие последние известия? |
| Get me a weekly paper | **Dastántye mnyé yizhinidyélnuyu gazyétu**<br>Достаньте мне еженедельную газету |
| Do you keep English papers? | **Yést u vass angléeskiye gazyéty?**<br>Есть у вас английские газеты? |
| Could you lend me your paper for a moment? | **Mózhitye adalzhéet mnyé váshu gazyétu na minútu?**<br>Можете одолжить мне вашу газету на минуту? |
| Have you a good Russian novel? | **Yést u vass kakóy-nibút kharóshy rússky ramán?**<br>Есть у вас какой-нибудь хороший русский роман? |
| Can you recommend a book by some modern author? | **Mózhitye vi rikomindavát knéegu kakóva-nibút savrimyénnava áftara?**<br>Можете вы рекомендовать книгу какого-нибудь современного автора? |
| Show me some books on Russian art | **Pakazhéetye mnyé knéegy pa rússkamu iskússtfu**<br>Покажите мне книги по русскому искусству |
| I need a good Russian-English pocket dictionary | **Mnyé núzhin kharóshy rússka-angléesky karmánny slavár**<br>Мне нужен хороший русско-английский карманный словарь |
| Have you a plan of Moscow? | **Yést u vass kárta Maskvíy?**<br>Есть у вас карта Москвы? |
| Can you recommend me a good guide-book? | **Mózhitye vi rikomindavát mnyé kharóshy putivadéetyil?**<br>Можете вы рекомендовать мне хороший путеводитель? |

Have you an illustrated guide-
book?

**Yést u vass illyustriróvanny
putivadéetyil?**

Есть у вас иллюстрированный
путеводитель?

Have you any postcards with
views of Moscow?

**Yést u vass atkrítky s véedamy
Maskvíy?**

Есть у вас открытки с видами
Москвы?

# Clothing and Footwear

|  |  |  |
|---|---|---|
| Masculine, men's | **Mushskáya** | Мужская |
| Feminine, women's | **Zhénskaya** | Женская |
| Children's | **Dyétskaya** | Детская |
| Ready-made | **Gatóvaya** | Готовая |
| Made to measure | **Na zakás** | На заказ |
| Overcoat (light, warm) | **Paltóh (lyókhkaye, tyóplaye)** | Пальто (лёгкое, тёплое) |
| Fur coat; skin coat | **Shúba** | Шуба |
| Raincoat (mackintosh) | **Plashch (makintósh, dazhdivéek)** | Плащ (макинтош, дождевик) |
| Hat | **Shlyápa** | Шляпа |
| 1 Man's (if brimmed) | 1 **Mushskáya (s palyámy)** | 1 Мужская (с полями) |
| 2 Woman's (generally) | 2 **Zhénskaya (vabshchéh)** | 2 Женская (вообще) |
| Felt | **Fyétravaya** | Фётровая |
| Straw | **Salóminnaya** | Соломенная |
| Summer | **Lyétnyaya** | Летняя |
| Fur hat (warm or soft) | **Shápka (tyóplaya éely myákhkaya)** | Шапка (тёплая или мягкая) |
| Peaked cap (soft, with peak) | **Kyépka (myákhkaya, s kazirkóm)** | Кёпка (мягкая, с козырьком) |
| (Head) scarf; head-square | **(Galavnóy) platók** | (Головной) платок |
| Scarf | **Sharff** | Шарф |
| Shawl | **Shal** | Шаль |
| Gloves | **Pirchátky** | Перчатки |
| Umbrella | **Zóntik** | Зонтик |
| Walking-stick | **Pálka** | Палка |
| Handkerchief | **(Nassavóy) platók** | (Носовой) платок |

## Men's wear (*Mushskáya adyézhda*; Мужска́я оде́жда)

| | | |
|---|---|---|
| Suit | **Kastyúm** | Костю́м |
| Jacket (of suit) | **Pidzhák** | Пиджа́к |
| Trousers | **Bryúky** | Брю́ки |
| Jacket (not part of suit) | **Kúrtka** | Ку́ртка |
| Dressing gown | **Khalát** | Хала́т |
| Belt | **Póyass** | По́яс |
| Tie | **Gálstuk** | Га́лстук |
| Socks | **Naskée** | Носки́ |
| Underpants | **Kalsóny** | Кальсо́ны |
| Vest | **Fufáyka** | Фуфа́йка |
| Shirt | **Rubáshka** | Руба́шка |
| Pyjamas | **Pizháma** | Пижа́ма |

## Women's clothing (*Zhénskaya adyézhda*; Же́нская оде́жда)

| | | |
|---|---|---|
| Dress | **Plátye** | Пла́тье |
| Suit | **Kastyúm** | Костю́м |
| Blouse | **Blúska** | Блу́зка |
| Skirt | **Yúpka** | Ю́бка |
| Slip; underskirt | **Néezhnyaya yúpka** | Ни́жняя юбка |
| Dressing gown | **Khalát (kapót)** | Хала́т (капо́т) |
| Stockings | **Chulkée** | Чулки́ |
| Brassière | **Léefchik** | Ли́фчик |
| Pants | **Pantalóny** | Пантало́ны |
| Nightdress | **Nachnáya rubáshka** | Ночна́я руба́шка |
| Tights | **Kalgótky** | Колго́тки |
| Boots (over ankle; laced) | **Botéenky** | Боти́нки |
| Knee boots | **Sapagée** | Сапоги́ |
| Shoes (ladies'); slippers: | **Túfly:** | Ту́фли: |
| Closed | zakrítiye | закры́тые |
| Open | atkrítye | откры́тые |
| Indoor (soft) | damáshniye (myákhkiye) | дома́шние (мя́гкие) |
| With low (high) heels | na néezkam (vissó-kam) kablukyéh | на ни́зком (высо́ком) каблуке́ |

| Suède | zámshiviye | зáмшевые |
|---|---|---|
| Leather footwear (canvas, rubber) | Óbuf kózhanaya (paruséenavaya, rizéenavaya) | Óбувь кóжаная (парусúновая, резúновая) |
| Soles | Padmyótky | Подмётки |
| Laces | Shnurkeé | Шнуркú |
| Shoe polish | Sapózhnaya mas | Сапóжная мазь |
| Sports wear: | Sparteévny kastyúm: | Спортúвный костюм: |
| Jacket; blazer | Kúrtka | Кýртка |
| Tee shirt | Máyka | Мáйка |
| Shorts | Trusseé | Трусы́ |
| Bathing costume | Kupálny kastyúm | Купáльный костюм |
| Fashion | Móda | Мóда |
| Design | Fassón (modyél) | Фасóн (модéль) |
| Material; fabric | Matyérya, tkan | Матéрия, ткань |
| Silk | Sholk | Шёлк |
| Velvet | Bárkhat | Бáрхат |
| Wool | Sherst | Шерсть |
| Linen | Palatnóh | Полотнó |
| Cotton fabric | Khlapchatabumázh-naya tkan | Хлопчатобумáж-ная ткань |
| Nylon fabric | Naylónavaya tkan | Найлóновая ткань |
| Plastic material | Matyérya eez plast-mássy | Матéрия из пласт-мáссы |
| Fur | Myékh | Мех |
| To dress | Adyivátsya | Одевáться |
| To undress | Razdyivátsya | Раздевáться |
| To put on | Nadyivát | Надевáть |
| To take off | Sneemát | Снимáть |
| To sew | Sheet (*perf.* s-sheet) | Шить (*perf.* сшить) |
| To make to measure | Sdyélat na zakás | Сдéлать на закáз |
| To repair | Chineét (*perf.* pachineét) | Чинúть (*perf.* починúть) |
| Colour | Tsvyét | Цвет |
| Red | Krássny | Крáсный |
| Blue (pale blue) | Seéniy (galubóy) | Сúний (голубóй) |
| Green | Zilyóny | Зелёный |

| Yellow | **Zhólty** | Жёлтый |
| Brown | **Karéechnivy** | Коричневый |
| Grey | **Syéry** | Серый |
| Black | **Chórny** | Чёрный |
| White | **Byély** | Белый |
| Purple | **Lilóvy** | Лиловый |
| Light | **Svyétly** | Светлый |
| Dark | **Tyómny** | Тёмный |

I want to order a suit

**Yá khachú zakazát kastyúm**

Я хочу заказать костюм

I prefer a tailored to a ready-made suit

**Yá pridpachitáyu kastyúm na zakás gatóvamu**

Я предпочитаю костюм на заказ готовому

What kind of material have you?

**Kakáya u vass matyérya?**

Какая у вас есть материя?

The sleeves are too short (long)

**Rukaváh sléeshkam kóratky (dléenny)**

Рукава слишком коротки (длинны)

The trousers are too long (short)

**Bryúky sléeshkam dléenny (kóratky)**

Брюки слишком длинны (коротки)

The lapels are too wide (narrow)

**Atvaróty sléeshkam shirakée (úsky)**

Отвороты слишком широки (узки)

The jacket fits badly (well)

**Pidzhák plókha (kharashóh) sidéet**

Пиджак плохо (хорошо) сидит

This suit is well cut

**État kastyúm kharóshiva pakróya**

Этот костюм хорошего покроя

This is a nice suit

**Éta kharóshy kastyúm**

Это хороший костюм

It's too big (small) for me

**On mnyé viléek (mal)**
Он мне вели́к (мал)

It can be altered

**Mózhna búdit piridyélat**
Мо́жно бу́дет переде́лать

Show me some silk dresses

**Pakazhéetye mnyé shólkaviye plátya**
Покажи́те мне шёлковые пла́тья

I need a warm woollen dress

**Mnyé núzhna tyóplaye shirstyinóye plátye**
Мне ну́жно тёплое шерстяно́е пла́тье

Have you any evening dresses?

**Yést u vass vichérniye plátya?**
Есть у вас вече́рние пла́тья?

The coat isn't warm enough

**Paltóh nidastátachna tyóplaye**
Пальто́ недоста́точно тёплое

I should like a red cap, a red shawl and some knitted woollen gloves

**Mnyé bi khatyélas imyét krássnuyu shápachku, krássnuyu shal ee vyázaniye shirstyiníye pirchátky**
Мне бы хоте́лось име́ть кра́сную ша́почку, кра́сную шаль и вя́заные шерстяны́е перча́тки

Wouldn't you prefer fur-lined gloves?

**Ni pridpachitáyitye ly vi pirchátky na mikhavóy padkládkye?**
Не предпочита́ете ли вы перча́тки на меховой подкла́дке?

A pair of green slippers lined with lamb's wool

**Pára zilyónikh túfel na baráshkavay padkládkye**
Па́ра зелёных ту́фель на бара́шковой подкла́дке

I want a pink petticoat

**Dáytye rózavuyu néezhnyuyu yúbku**
Да́йте ро́зовую ни́жнюю ю́бку

The hat is too big (small) for me

**Shlyápa mnyé vilikáh (maláh)**
Шля́па мне велика́ (мала́)

| | |
|---|---|
| Show me some coloured shirts | **Pakazhéetye mnyé tsvitníye rubáshky** |
| | Покажи́те мне цветны́е руба́шки |
| I like coloured socks | **Mnyé nrávitsya tsvitníye nasskeé** |
| | Мне нра́вятся цветны́е носки́ |
| The woollen socks have shrunk | **Shirstyiníye nasskeé syély** |
| | Шерстяны́е носки́ се́ли |
| The colour has run | **Tsvyét slinyál** |
| | Цвет слиня́л |
| Do you prefer brown or black shoes? | **Vi pridpachitáyitye kareéchniviye éely chórniye batéenky?** |
| | Вы предпочита́ете кори́чневые и́ли чёрные боти́нки? |
| I must try them on | **Yá dólzhin yéekh primyérit** |
| | Я до́лжен их приме́рить |
| The shoes are too narrow (broad) | **Batéenky sléeshkam úsky (shirakeé)** |
| | Боти́нки сли́шком у́зки (широки́) |
| The toe-cap pinches | **Nassók zhmyót** |
| | Носо́к жмёт |
| Give me a pair of brown laces | **Dáytye páru kareéchnivikh shnurkóf** |
| | Да́йте па́ру кори́чневых шнурко́в |
| I must have my grey hat cleaned | **Yá dólzhin atdát f chéestku svayeé syéruyu shlyápu** |
| | Я до́лжен отда́ть в чи́стку свою́ се́рую шля́пу |
| The suit must be repaired; the lining is torn | **Kastyúm náda pachineét, padkládka pórvana** |
| | Костю́м на́до почини́ть, подкла́дка по́рвана |
| Send the shoes to be mended; they need new soles | **Atdáytye pachineét batéenky, nuzhneé nóviye padmyótky** |
| | Отда́йте почин—́ть боти́нки, нужны́ но́вые подмётки |

These shoes need new heels

**Náda padbéet kablukée étikh túfel**

Надо подби́ть каблуки́ э́тих ту́фель

# At the Hairdresser

| Haircut | **Prichóska** | Причёска |
| Permanent wave | **Zavéevka pirmanyént** | Завивка перманент |
| To cut, trim | **Streech** | Стричь |
| To shampoo | **Mwít** | Мыть |
| To set | **Ulazhéet (ukládivat) vólassy** | Уложить (укладывать) волосы |
| (Safety) razor | **(Bizapásnaya) bréetva** | (Безопасная) бритва |
| Razor blade | **Lyézviye bréetvy** | Лезвие бритвы |
| Hairgrip | **Pryázhka dlyá valóss** | Пряжка для волос |
| Parting | **Prabór** | Пробор |
| Curl | **Lókan** | Локон |
| Comb | **Gribyónka** | Гребёнка |
| Brush | **Shchótka** | Щётка |
| To do one's hair | **Prichóssivatsya** | Причёсываться |
| To shave (oneself) | **Bréets(ya)** | Брить(ся) |
| To lather | **Namwílivat** | Намыливать |

Is there a men's hairdresser (barber) near here?

**Yést zdyés bléezka mushskáya parikmákhirskaya?**

Есть здесь близко мужская парикмахерская?

Can you recommend a ladies' hairdresser?

**Mózhitye vi rikamindavát dámskava parikmákhira?**

Можете вы рекомендовать дамского парикмахера?

Give me a haircut

**Padstrigéetye mnyé vólossy**

Подстригите мне волосы

Not too short

**Ni sléeshkam kóratka**

Не слишком коротко

Only a trim (clean it up)

**Tólka padravnyáytye**

Только подровняйте

| | |
|---|---|
| Don't cut too much off | **Ni srizáytye sléeshkam mnóga**<br>Не срезáйте слúшком мнóго |
| Give me a shave | **Pabryeytye minyá**<br>Побрéйте меня́ |
| I'd like a shampoo | **Mnyé bi khatyélas vímwit vólassy**<br>Мне бы хотéлось вы́мыть<br>вóлосы |
| Which side is your parting? | **S kakóy staranée u vass prabór?**<br>С какóй сторонь́ у вас пробóр? |
| I want a shampoo and a set | **Yá khachú, shtóby vi mnyé<br>vímwily ee ulazhéely vólassy**<br>Я хочý, чтóбы вы мне вы́мыли<br>и уложи́ли вóлосы |
| I'd like to try a new style | **Mnyé bi khatyélas prichisátsya<br>pa-nóvamu**<br>Мне бы хотéлось причесáться<br>по-нóвому |
| This style is old-fashioned | **Éta prichóska ni módnaya**<br>Э́та причёска не мóдная |
| Do you want curls? | **Vi khatéetye lókany?**<br>Вы хоти́те лóконы? |
| Would you like your hair<br>lightened? | **Khatéetye víbilit vólassy?**<br>Хоти́те вы́белить вóлосы? |
| I should like a perm | **Yá khachú sdyélat pirmanyént**<br>Я хочý сдéлать перманéнт |
| How much will it cost? | **Skólka éta búdyit stóit?**<br>Скóлько э́то бýдет стóить? |
| Can I come tomorrow for a<br>perm? | **Magú yá preetée záftra dlyá<br>pirmanyénta?**<br>Могý я прийти́ зáвтра для<br>перманéнта? |
| Do you do manicures<br>(pedicures)? | **U vass mózhna sdyélat manikyúr<br>(pidikyúr)?**<br>У вас мóжно сдéлать маникю́р<br>(педикю́р)? |

# Entertainment

The service bureau may be able to help with tickets for the theatre and the circus. Visitors to Moscow should visit the Bolshoi theatre and, perhaps, attend a concert, gymnastic or figure-skating display. Tickets for the Bolshoi are usually available at the *Excursion Bureau* of the Intourist Hotel in Gorky Street. (Monday afternoon is the best time to apply, but they can usually offer something all week.)

## The theatre

It is virtually impossible to get tickets for the most successful productions in the 'straight' theatre, but the tourist with an interest in Russian theatrical tradition might like to visit the *Moscow Arts Theatre* (the old building), and see a classic acted in the classical manner. This theatre is no longer fashionable and there is no problem buying tickets. A serious attempt should also be made to see a performance at the *puppet theatre*.

At the theatre you must leave your outer clothing in the cloakroom. When you give in your things you will be offered opera glasses. They cost 30 kopecks and are worth taking because, after the performance, if you have opera glasses you do not have to stand in the queue for your coats, you go straight to the head of the queue, holding your opera glasses conspicuously. Inside the theatre, as you pass along the row to your seat, it is considered polite to face the person you are passing.

Also, at the theatre, one can often find Russian delicacies like caviar and smoked fish on sale. These are difficult to obtain elsewhere.

Outside the theatre one may be approached by Russians who want to buy a ticket for that performance. They ask: 'U vass nyét léeshniva?' ('Have you a spare ticket?'). These tickets change hands at their normal cost.

| | | |
|---|---|---|
| Theatre | **Tiátr** | Теа́тр |
| Opera-house | **Tiátr ópiry** | Теа́тр о́перы |
| Entrance | **Padyézd** | Подъе́зд |
| Vestibule | **Vistibyúl** | Вестибю́ль |
| Box-office | **Kássa** | Ка́сса |
| Advance booking | **Pridvaréetilnaya pradázha bilyétaf** | Предвари́тельная прода́жа биле́тов |
| Evening (afternoon) performance | **Vichérny (dnivnóy) spiktákl** | Вече́рний (дневно́й) спекта́кль |
| Matinée | **Útrinnik** | У́тренник |
| Cloakroom | **Gardiróp** | Гардеро́б |
| Toilet | **Twalyét (ubórnaya)** | Туале́т (убо́рная) |
| Foyer | **Foyéh** | Фойе́ |
| Refreshment room; buffet | **Buffyét** | Буфе́т |
| Smoking room | **Kuréetilnaya kómnata** | Кури́тельная ко́мната |
| Emergency exit | **Zapasnóy víkhat** | Запасно́й вы́ход |
| Attendant; usherette | **Bilyetyórsha** | Билете́рша |
| Auditorium | **Zréetilny zal** | Зри́тельный зал |
| Stage | **Stséna** | Сце́на |
| Curtain | **Zánavis** | За́навес |
| Wings | **Kuléessy** | Кули́сы |
| Stage setting; scene | **Dekarátsya** | Декора́ция |
| Box | **Lózha** | Ло́жа |
| Stalls | **Kryésla** | Кре́сла |
| Amphitheatre; pit | **Partér (amfitiátr)** | Парте́р (амфитеа́тр) |
| Dress circle; circle | **Beletázh (pyérvy yáruss)** | Бельэта́ж (пе́рвый я́рус) |
| Balcony | **Balkón** | Балко́н |
| Gallery | **Galaryéya** | Галере́я |
| Performance | **Pridstavlyénya (spiktákl)** | Представле́ние (спекта́кль) |

| Tragedy | **Tragyédiya** | Траге́дия |
|---|---|---|
| Comedy | **Kamyédiya** | Коме́дия |
| Play | **Dráma, pyéssa** | Дра́ма, пье́са |
| One-act play | **Adna-áktnaya pyéssa** | Одноа́ктная пье́са |
| Act | **Dyéystviye (akt)** | Де́йствие (акт) |
| Scene | **Yivlyénye (kartéena, stséna)** | Явле́ние (карти́на, сце́на) |
| Interval | **Antrákt** | Антра́кт |
| Author | **Áftar** | А́втор |
| Dramatist | **Dramatúrg** | Драмату́рг |
| Poet | **Paét** | Поэ́т |
| Actor | **Aktyór** | Актёр |
| Actress | **Aktréessa** | Актри́са |
| Producer | **Rizhissyór** | Режиссёр |
| Rôle; part | **Rohl** | Роль |
| Prompter | **Sufflyór** | Суфлёр |
| Singer | **Pivyéts (pivéetsa)** | Певе́ц (певи́ца) |
| Conductor | **Dirizhór** | Дирижёр |
| To play | **Igrát** | Игра́ть |
| To see; to watch | **Smatryét** | Смотре́ть |
| Concert | **Kantsért** | Конце́рт |
| Concert hall | **Kantsértny zal** | Конце́ртный зал |
| Grand piano | **Rayál** | Роя́ль |
| Pianist | **Pianéest(ka)** | Пиани́ст(ка) |
| Violin | **Skréepka** | Скри́пка |
| Violinist | **Skripách(ka)** | Скрипа́ч(ка) |
| Cello | **Vialanchél** | Виолонче́ль |
| Double bass | **Kantrabáss** | Контраба́с |
| Flute | **Fléyta** | Фле́йта |
| Trumpet | **Trubáh** | Труба́ |
| Harp | **Árfa** | А́рфа |
| Drum | **Barabán** | Бараба́н |
| Orchestra (string, wind, symphony) | **Arkyéstr (strúnny, dukhavóy, simfanéechesky)** | Орке́стр (стру́нный, духово́й, симфони́ческий) |
| Chamber music | **Kámirnaya múzika** | Ка́мерная му́зыка |
| Applause | **Apladismyénty** | Аплодисме́нты |

| To applaud; to clap | **Apladeéravat (khlópat)** | Аплоди́ровать (хло́пать) |
| Ballet | **Balyét** | Бале́т |
| Ballerina | **Balireéna (tantsóvshchitsa)** | Балери́на (танцо́вщица) |
| Male dancer | **Tantsóvshchik** | Танцо́вщик |

What is on at the theatre today? — **Shto sivódnya idyót f tiátrye?**
Что сего́дня идёт в теа́тре?

There's a tragedy at the National Theatre — **V gasudárstvinnam tiátrye idyót tragyédya**
В госуда́рственном теа́тре идёт траге́дия

I'd like to see a comedy — **Mnyé bi khatyélas pasmatryét kamyédyu**
Мне бы хоте́лось посмотре́ть коме́дию

Would you like to go to the opera (ballet)? — **Khateétye payteé v ópiru (na balyét)?**
Хоти́те пойти́ в о́перу (на бале́т)?

They are showing the ballet *Swan Lake* today — **Sivódnya dayút balyét 'Libideénaye ózira'**
Сего́дня даю́т бале́т «Лебеди́ное о́зеро»

Tomorrow is the last performance of the *Sleeping Beauty* — **Záftra paslyédnyeye pridstavlyénye 'Spyáshchey krassávitsy'**
За́втра после́днее представле́ние «Спя́щей краса́вицы»

What is on at the Bolshoi? — **Shto idyót v Balshóm tiátrye?**
Что идёт в «Большо́м теа́тре»?

Who is taking part in the opera? — **Kto uchástvuyit v ópirye?**
Кто уча́ствует в о́пере?

Do you want to go to a circus? — **Khateétye payteé f tsírk?**
Хоти́те пойти́ в цирк?

I don't like acrobats — **Yá ni lyublyú akrabátaf**
Я не люблю́ акроба́тов

When does the performance (concert) begin? | **Kagdá nachináyitsya pridstavlyé-nye (kantsért)?**
Когда́ начина́ется представле́-ние (конце́рт)?

If we want to arrive in time we must take a taxi | **Yésly mi khateém papást vó-vremya, mi dalzhneé vzyát takseé**
Е́сли мы хоти́м попа́сть во́-время, мы должны́ взять такси́

We are late | **Mi apazdály**
Мы опозда́ли

The second act has started | **Idyót ftaróy akt**
Идёт второ́й акт

Late-comers must wait till an interval | **Vkhadeét vo vryémya dyéystvya nilzyá**
Входи́ть во вре́мя де́йствия нельзя́

We shall not get tickets | **Mi ni palúchim bilyétaf**
Мы не полу́чим биле́тов

Tickets are sold out | **Vsyé bilyéty paspródany**
Все биле́ты распро́даны

There is only standing room | **Astális tólka stayáchiye mistáh**
Оста́лись то́лько стоя́чие места́

Tickets must be purchased in advance | **Bilyéty náda brát zarányeye**
Биле́ты на́до брать зара́нее

When is the advance booking office open? | **Kagdá atkríta kássa pridvareé-tilnay pradázhy?**
Когда́ откры́та ка́сса пред-вари́тельной прода́жи?

You have to queue | **Náda stayát v óchiridy**
На́до стоя́ть в о́череди

Can I order tickets by telephone? | **Magú yá zakazát bilyéty pa tilifónu?**
Могу́ я заказа́ть биле́ты по телефо́ну?

How much do front-row seats cost? (Seat in the Balcony, Upper Circle, Gallery?)

**Skólka stóyat pyérviye ridée? (myésta na balkónye, vo ftaróm yárussye, na galiryéye?)**

Ско́лько сто́ят пе́рвые ряды́? (ме́сто на балко́не, во второ́м я́русе, на галере́е?)

Show me where these seats are on the plan

**Pakazhéetye pa plánu, gdyé éty mistáh**

Покажи́те по пла́ну, где э́ти места́

Can one see well from there?

**Atsyúda kharashóh véedna?**

Отсю́да хорошо́ ви́дно?

Two amphitheatre stalls, preferably in the middle (near the gangway)

**Dva kryésla f partérye, yésly vazmózhna f sirideénye (ókala prakhóda)**

Два кре́сла в парте́ре, е́сли возмо́жно в середи́не (о́коло прохо́да)

You had better take tickets for the Circle (Gallery)

**Lúchshe vazméetye bilyéty v bilitázhe (na balkónye)**

Лу́чше возьми́те биле́ты в бельэта́же (на балко́не)

Which floor is the Balcony (Gallery) on?

**F kakóm yárussye balkón (galiryéya)?**

В како́м я́русе балко́н (галере́я)?

Wait for me by the entrance (in the vestibule, by the desk)

**Zhdéetye minyá u padyézda (v vistibyúlye, u kássy)**

Жди́те меня́ у подъе́зда (в вестибю́ле, у ка́ссы)

Do you want a programme and opera glasses?

**Khatéetye pragrámmu ee binókl?**

Хоти́те програ́мму и бино́кль?

How long is the interval?

**Skólka pradalzháyitsya antrákt?**

Ско́лько продолжа́ется антра́кт?

Can we have tea or coffee in the interval?

**Mózhna palucheét cháy éely kófye vo vryémya antrákta?**

Мо́жно получи́ть чай и́ли ко́фе во вре́мя антра́кта?

Only in the buffet

**Tólka v buffyétye**

То́лько в буфе́те

I've lost my cloakroom ticket (check)

**Yá patiryál nomirók gardiróba**

Я потеря́л номеро́к гардеро́ба

The actors are very good

**Aktyóry kharashóh igráyut**

Актёры хорошо́ игра́ют

The play is enthralling (boring)

**Pyéssa intiryésnaya (skúshnaya)**

Пье́са захва́тывающая (ску́чная)

The production is poor

**Pastanófka plakháya**

Постано́вка плоха́я

Yesterday was the first night

**Fchiráh bwiláh primyéra**

Вчера́ была́ премье́ра

When was it first performed?

**Kagdá bwila pyérvaye pridstavlyénye?**

Когда́ бы́ло пе́рвое представле́ние?

I have two tickets for today's concert

**U minyá dva bilyéta na sivódnishny kantsért**

У меня́ два биле́та на сего́дняшний конце́рт

Who is playing in the concert?

**Kto uchástvuyit f kantsértye?**

Кто уча́ствует в конце́рте?

Do you prefer classical or light music?

**Vi pridpachitáyitye klasséechiskuyu éely lyókhkuyu múziku?**

Вы предпочита́ете класси́ческую и́ли лёгкую му́зыку?

Do you like chamber music?

**Vi lyúbitye kámirnuyu múziku?**

Вы лю́бите ка́мерную му́зыку?

This orchestra is famous

**État arkyéstr znaminéety**

Э́тот орке́стр знамени́тый

## The cinema

Performances begin at 10 am and continue (separate performances only) until midnight. Seats are very cheap in all cinemas.

| | | |
|---|---|---|
| Cinema | **Keenatiátr (keenóh)** | Кинотеа́тр (кино́) |
| Film | **Keenaféelm (féelm)** | Кинофи́льм (фильм) |
| Screen | **Ekrán** | Экра́н |
| Sound film | **Zvukavóy féelm** | Звуково́й фильм |
| Artistic | **Khudózhistvinny** | Худо́жественный |
| Documentary | **Dakumintálny** | Документа́льный |
| Popular science | **Naúchna-papulyárny** | Нау́чно-популя́рный |
| Adventure | **Priklyuchénchisky** | Приключе́нческий |
| Animated cartoon | **Multiplikatsyónny** | Мультипликацио́нный |
| Caricature | **Karikatúra** | Карикату́ра |
| Newsreel | **Keenakhrónika** | Кинохро́ника |
| Producer | **Keenarizhissyór** | Кинорежиссёр |
| Star | **Zvizdáh** | Звезда́ |
| Production | **Pastanófka** | Постано́вка |
| Film studio | **Keenastúdya** | Киносту́дия |
| To film | **Zasnyát** | Засня́ть |
| Close-up | **Krúpny plan** | Кру́пный план |
| A frame; a still | **Kadr** | Кадр |

| | |
|---|---|
| When is the next performance? | **Kagdá slyédushchy seánss?** |
| | Когда́ сле́дующий сеа́нс? |
| The newsreel is at 3.30 | **Khróniku pakázivayut f tree tréetsat** |
| | Хро́нику пока́зывают в 3.30 |
| What is on at the big cinema? | **Shto pakázivayut v balshóm keenóh?** |
| | Что пока́зывают в большо́м кино́? |
| There's a new film | **Idyót nóvy féelm** |
| | Идёт но́вый фильм |

| | |
|---|---|
| Is it a serious film or a comedy? | **Éta siryóznaya kartéena éely kaméechiskaya?**<br>Это серьёзная карти́на и́ли коми́ческая? |
| I should like to see a topical film | **Yá bi khatyél véedit zlabadnyévny féelm**<br>Я бы хоте́л ви́деть злободне́в-ный фильм |
| This is a beautiful colour film | **Éta prikrásny tsvitnóy féelm**<br>Это прекра́сный цветно́й фильм |
| Do you want to see a good animal film? | **Khatéetye pasmatryét kharóshuyu kartéenu eez zhéezny zhivótnikh?**<br>Хоти́те посмотре́ть хоро́шую карти́ну из жи́зни живо́тных? |
| We'd better sit at the back | **Nam lúchshe syést szády**<br>Нам лу́чше сесть сза́ди |
| Is there an emergency exit? | **Yést zapasnóy víkhat?**<br>Есть запасно́й вы́ход? |
| Can we book in advance? | **Mózhna vzyát bilyéty zarányeye?**<br>Мо́жно взять биле́ты зара́нее? |
| You must collect the tickets half an hour before the perform-ance begins | **Náda zabrát bilyéty za palchassáh da nachála seánssa**<br>На́до забра́ть биле́ты за полчаса́ до нача́ла сеа́нса |
| Come early. There'll be a long queue | **Prikhadéetye ránshe. Búdyit balsháya óchirit**<br>Приходи́те ра́ньше. Бу́дет больша́я о́чередь |

# Medical Treatment

| | | |
|---|---|---|
| Head | **Galaváh** | Голова́ |
| Skull | **Chérip** | Че́реп |
| Face | **Litsóh** | Лицо́ |
| Forehead | **Lop** | Лоб |
| Eye | **Glas** | Глаз |
| Eyelid | **Vyéka** | Ве́ко |
| Eyebrow | **Broff** | Бровь |
| Ear | **Úkha** | У́хо |
| Nose | **Noss** | Нос |
| Mouth | **Rot** | Рот |
| Lip | **Gubáh** | Губа́ |
| Cheek | **Shchikáh** | Щека́ |
| Chin | **Padbaródok** | Подборо́док |
| Jaw | **Chélyist** | Че́люсть |
| Tooth | **Zup** | Зуб |
| Gum | **Disnáh** | Десна́ |
| Tongue | **Yazík** | Язы́к |
| Neck | **Shéya** | Ше́я |
| Throat | **Górla** | Го́рло |
| Tonsil | **Mindalivéednaya zhilizáh** | Миндалеви́дная железа́ |
| Gland | **Zhilizáh** | Железа́ |
| Hair | **Vólassy** | Во́лосы |
| Skin | **Kózha** | Ко́жа |
| Body | **Tyéla** | Те́ло |
| Bone | **Kost** | Кость |
| Rib | **Ribróh** | Ребро́ |
| Spine | **Spinnóy khribyét** | Спинно́й хребе́т |
| Chest | **Grut** | Грудь |
| Belly | **Zhivót** | Живо́т |
| Lung | **Lyókhkaye** | Лёгкое |
| Heart | **Syérdtse** | Се́рдце |

| Bowels | **Kishkée** | Кишки́ |
| Stomach | **Zhilyúdak** | Желу́док |
| Shoulder | **Plichóh** | Плечо́ |
| Arm | **Rukáh** | Рука́ |
| Elbow | **Lókat** | Ло́коть |
| Hand | **Rukáh** | Рука́ |
| Wrist | **Zapyástye** | Запя́стье |
| Finger | **Pálits** | Па́лец |
| Thumb | **Balshóy pálits** | Большо́й па́лец |
| Nail | **Nógat** | Но́готь |
| Leg | **Nagáh** | Нога́ |
| Hip; thigh | **Bidróh** | Бедро́ |
| Knee | **Kalyéna** | Коле́но |
| Ankle | **Shchéekalka (ladíshka)** | Щи́колка (лоды́жка) |
| Foot | **Stupnyáh** | Ступня́ |
| Toe | **Pálits na nogyéh** | Па́лец на ноге́ |
| Blood | **Krof** | Кровь |
| Vein | **Vyéna** | Ве́на |
| Illness; disease | **Balyézn** | Боле́знь |
| Pain | **Bol** | Боль |
| Headache | **Galavnáya bol** | Головна́я боль |
| Cold | **Prastúda** | Просту́да |
| Cough | **Káshil** | Ка́шель |
| Cold in the head | **Nássmark** | На́сморк |
| Influenza | **Greep** | Грипп |
| Inflammation | **Vaspalyénye** | Воспале́ние |
| Pneumonia | **Vaspalyénye lyókhkikh** | Воспале́ние лёгких |
| Tonsilitis | **Angéena** | Анги́на |
| Faint | **Óbmarak** | О́бморок |
| Giddiness | **Galavakruzhénye** | Головокруже́ние |
| Loss of consciousness | **Patyérya saznánya** | Поте́ря созна́ния |
| Sickness; nausea | **Tashnatáh** | Тошнота́ |
| Vomiting | **Rvóta** | Рво́та |
| Diarrhoea | **Panóss** | Поно́с |

| Constipation | **Zapór** | Запо́р |
| Indigestion | **Nisvaryénye zhilúdka** | Несваре́ние желу́дка |
| Fracture | **Pirilóm kósty** | Перело́м ко́сти |
| Dislocation | **Vívikh** | Вы́вих |
| Sprain | **Rastyizhénye svyázok** | Растяже́ние связок |
| Cut | **Paryés** | Поре́з |
| Burn; scald | **Azhók** | Ожо́г |
| Splinter | **Zanóza** | Зано́за |
| Corn | **Mazól** | Мозо́ль |
| Bruise | **Sinyák** | Синя́к |
| Abscess | **Naгív** | Нары́в |
| Boil | **Furúnkul** | Фуру́нкул |
| Ulcer | **Yázva** | Я́зва |
| Doctor | **Vrach (dóktar)** | Врач (до́ктор) |
| Dentist (Eye, Ear specialist) | **Zubnóy (glaznóy, ushnóy) vrach** | Зубно́й (глазно́й, ушно́й) врач |
| Specialist | **Spitsaléest** | Специали́ст |
| Surgeon | **Khirúrg** | Хиру́рг |
| Medical examination | **Miditséensky asmótr** | Медици́нский осмо́тр |
| Treatment | **Lichénye** | Лече́ние |
| To treat | **Lichéet** | Лечи́ть |
| To cure | **Vílichit** | Вы́лечить |
| To anaesthetise | **Anistizéeravat (davát narkós)** | Анестези́ровать (дава́ть нарко́з) |
| Medicine | **Likárstva** | Лека́рство |
| Prescription | **Ritsépt** | Реце́пт |
| Ambulance | **Aftamabéel skóray pómashchy** | Автомоби́ль ско́рой по́мощи |
| Nurse | **(Mid)sistráh** | (Мед)сестра́ |
| Toothache | **Zubnáya bol** | Зубна́я боль |
| To extract | **Udalyát** | Удаля́ть |
| To fill | **Plambiravát** | Пломбирова́ть |

## At the doctor

What are Dr. . . .'s hours for consultation?

**F katóram chassú prinimáyit dóktar . . .?**

В котóром часý принимáет дóктор . . .?

Send for the doctor

**Pashléetye za dóktaram**

Пошлúте за дóктором

Telephone for the doctor

**Vizavéetye dóktara pa tilifónu**

Вызовúте дóктора по телефóну

I'll go to him myself

**Yá sam payédu k nimú**

Я сам поéду к немý

Find out when he can see me

**Uznáytye kagdá on mózhit préenyit minyá**

Узнáйте, когдá он мóжет прúнять меня́

Send for First Aid (an ambulance)

**Vizavéetye skóruyu pómashch**

Вызовúте скóрую пóмощь

What is the matter?

**Shto s vámy?**

Что с вáми?

What are your (his, her) symptoms?

**Shto u vass (u nivóh, u nyiyóh) baléet?**

Что у вас (у негó, у неё) болúт?

Where is your pain?

**Gdyé u vass bol?**

Где у вас боль?

Does it hurt here?

**Zdyés bólna?**

Здесь бóльно?

I have cut my finger

**Yá paryézal pálits**

Я порéзал пáлец

I've burnt my arm (leg)

**Yá abzhók rúku (nógu)**

Я обжёг рýку (нóгу)

Something got into my eye

**Shtó-ta mnyé papála v glas**

Чтó-то попáло мне в глаз

I don't feel well

**Yá plókha sibyáh chúfstvuyu**

Я плóхо себя́ чýвствую

I feel very ill

**Mnyé óchin plókha**

Мне óчень плóхо

| | |
|---|---|
| I feel sick | **Minyá tashneét**<br>Меня тошнит |
| My head is giddy | **U minyá krúzhitsya galaváh**<br>У меня кружится голова |
| I feel very weak | **U minyá balsháya slábast**<br>У меня большая слабость |
| My throat hurts | **U minyá baleét górla**<br>У меня болит горло |
| I have a terrible cold (cough) | **U minyá seélny nássmark (káshil)**<br>У меня сильный насморк (кашель) |
| My (his, her) head (stomach) aches | **U minyá (u nivóh, u nyiyóh) baleét galaváh (zhivót)**<br>У меня (у него, у неё) болит голова (живот) |
| I have a pain in my stomach (chest, throat, foot) | **U minyá bol v zhilúdkye (v grudeé, v górlye, f stupnyéh)**<br>У меня боль в желудке (в груди, в горле, в ступне) |
| I must examine you | **Yá dólzhin asmatryét vass**<br>Я должен осмотреть вас |
| I must take your temperature | **Yá smyéryu u vass timpiratúru**<br>Я смерю у вас температуру |
| You are very (rather) feverish | **U vass (ni)balshóy zhar**<br>У вас (не)большой жар |
| You have only caught a cold | **U vass tólka prastúda**<br>У вас только простуда |
| I shall prescribe you a gargle (some pills, tablets, medicine) | **Yá prapishú vam palaskánye (pilyúly, tablyétky, likárstva)**<br>Я пропишу вам полоскание (пилюли, таблетки, лекарство) |
| You must gargle and take the cough mixture | **Vi dalzhneé palaskát górla ee prinimát mikstúru at káshlya**<br>Вы должны полоскать горло и принимать микстуру от кашля |

| | |
|---|---|
| Take the pills three times a day | **Prinimáytye pilyúly tree ráza v dyén**<br>Принима́йте пилю́ли три ра́за в день |
| Don't go out for two or three days | **Ni vikhadéetye na úlitsu dva-tree dnyá**<br>Не выходи́те на у́лицу два-три дня |
| Let me know if there's no improvement (come and see me again) | **Yésly ni búdyit lúchshe dáytye mnyé znat (prikhadéetye ka mnyé apyát)**<br>Éсли не бу́дет лу́чше, да́йте мне знать (приходи́те ко мне опя́ть) |
| Your throat is inflamed | **U vass vaspalyénye górla**<br>У вас воспале́ние го́рла |
| Your tonsils are swollen | **U vass apúkhly zhélizy**<br>У вас опу́хли же́лезы |
| Is your digestion all right? | **F paryátkye ly u vass pishi-varyénye?**<br>В поря́дке ли у вас пище-варе́ние? |
| The medicine did no good | **Likárstva ni pamaglóh**<br>Лека́рство не помогло́ |
| How do you (does he, she) feel now? | **Kak on, anáh (vi) sibyáh tipyér chúfstvuyit(ye)?**<br>Как он, она́ (вы) себя́ тепе́рь чу́вствует(е)? |
| I am (he, she is) better (worse) | **Mnyé (yimú, yéy) lúchshe (khúzhe)**<br>Мне (ему́, ей) лу́чше (ху́же) |
| The heartburn (diarrhoea, vomiting, constipation, pain) continues | **Izhóga (panóss, rvóta, zapór, bol) pradalzháyitsya**<br>Изжо́га (поно́с, рво́та, запо́р, боль) продолжа́ется |

You must go into hospital (for investigation, for observation)

**Vam náda lyéch v balnéetsu (dlyá islyédavanya, dlyá nablyu-dyénya)**

Вам на́до лечь в больни́цу (для иссле́дования, для наблю-де́ния)

She has pneumonia (bronchitis, measles, scarlet-fever, typhoid, high [low] blood pressure, heart attack)

**U nyiyóh vaspalyénye lyókhkikh (brankhéet, kor, skarlatéena, bryushnóy teéff, pavíshinaye [panéezhinnaye] davlyénye króvy, sirdyéchny pripádak)**

У неё воспале́ние лёгких (бронхи́т, корь, скарлати́на, брюшно́й тиф, повы́шенное [пони́женное] давле́ние кро́ви, серде́чный припа́док)

The illness got worse (better)

**Balyézn ukhúdshilas (ulúchshilas)**

Боле́знь уху́дшилась (улу́чши-лась)

He was injured in an accident

**On paluchéel pavrizhdyénye pree aváriy**

Он получи́л поврежде́ние при ава́рии

He was run over

**On papál pad mashéenu**

Он попа́л под маши́ну

He was knocked over by a motor-cycle

**On bwil sbéet s nok matatséeklam**

Он был сбит с ног мотоци́клом

I fell on the stairs

**Yá upál na lyéstnitse**

Я упа́л на ле́стнице

You have broken your arm

**Vi slamály sibyéh rúku**

Вы слома́ли себе́ ру́ку

You have dislocated your ankle

**Vi vívikhnuly sibyéh ladíshku**

Вы вы́вихнули себе́ лоды́жку

You only have a sprain

**U vass tólka rastyizhénye svyázak**

У вас то́лько растяже́ние свя́зок

| | |
|---|---|
| We'll strap it up for you | **Mi sdyélayim vam pirivyázku**<br>Мы сделаем вам перевязку |
| She (he) has fainted | **U nyiyóh óbmarak (u nivóh óbmarak)**<br>У неё обморок (у него обморок) |
| She (he) has lost consciousness | **Anáh (on) patiryála saznánye**<br>Она (он) потеряла сознание |
| She (he) has come round | **Anáh prishláh (on prishól) f sibyáh**<br>Она пришла (он пришёл) в себя |
| I must bandage your foot | **Yá dólzhin pirivyizát vam nógu**<br>Я должен перевязать вам ногу |
| You are badly bruised | **U vass balshéeye sinyakée**<br>У вас большие синяки |
| I can't hear very well | **Yá plókha slíshu**<br>Я плохо слышу |
| My ear hurts | **U minyá baléet úkha**<br>У меня болит ухо |
| I am deaf | **Yá glukhóy**<br>Я глухой |
| You must consult an ear specialist | **Vi dalzhnée abratéetsya k ushnómu spitsaléestu**<br>Вы должны обратиться к ушному специалисту |
| Something has happened to my eye(s) | **U minyá shtó-ta sluchéelas z glázam (z glázámy)**<br>У меня что-то случилось с глазом (с глазами) |
| The eye is (eyes are) running | **Glas slizéetsya (glazá slizátsya)**<br>Глаз слезится (глаза слезятся) |
| It hurts to use my eyes | **Mnyé bólna smatryét**<br>Мне больно смотреть |

# At the dentist

| | |
|---|---|
| Please go into the surgery | **Pazhálusta, praydéetye f kabinyét**<br>Пожалуйста, пройдите в кабинет |
| This molar (front) tooth aches | **U minyá baléet état karinnóy zup (piryédny zup)**<br>У меня болит этот коренной зуб (передний зуб) |
| My stopping fell out | **U minyá vípala plómba**<br>У меня выпала пломба |
| It must be filled | **Yivóh náda zaplambiravát**<br>Его надо запломбировать |
| You must have a gold crown on the tooth | **Vam pridyótsya pastávit na zup zalatúyu karónku**<br>Вам придётся поставить на зуб золотую коронку |
| I must take the tooth out | **Zup náda udaléet (vídirnut)**<br>Зуб надо удалить (выдернуть) |
| The root is decayed | **Kórin zgnéel**<br>Корень сгнил |
| I shall give you a local anaesthetic | **Yá vam dam myéstny narkós**<br>Я вам дам местный наркоз |
| The gums are bleeding | **Dyóssny kravatachát**<br>Дёсны кровоточат |
| You have an abscess on the gum | **U vass naṛív na dissnyéh**<br>У вас нарыв на десне |

# Correspondence

|  |  |  |
|---|---|---|
| Letter | Peessmóh | Письмо́ |
| Business letter | Dilavóye peessmóh | Делово́е письмо́ |
| Postcard | Atkrítka | Откры́тка |
| Picture postcard | Atkrítka s véedam | Откры́тка с ви́дом |
| Handwriting | Póchirk | По́черк |
| Fountain pen | Aftarúchka | Авторучка |
| Pencil | Karandásh | Каранда́ш |
| Coloured pencil | Tsvitnóy karandásh | Цветно́й каранда́ш |
| Paper | Bumága | Бума́га |
| Note-paper | Pachtóvaya bumága | Почто́вая бума́га |
| Envelope | Kanvyért | Конве́рт |
| Writing pad | Blaknót | Блокно́т |
| Blotting-paper | Pramakátilnaya bumága | Промока́тельная бума́га |
| Ink | Chirnéela | Черни́ла |
| Stationer's | Kantstaváry (Kantsilyárskiye taváry) | Канцтова́ры (Канцеля́рские това́ры) |
| Shorthand | Stinográfya | Стеногра́фия |
| Typewriter | Péeshushchaya mashéenka | Пи́шущая маши́нка |
| Carbon-paper | Kapiraválnaya bumága | Копирова́льная бума́га |
| Sender | Atpravéetil | Отправи́тель |
| Addressee | Adrissát | Адреса́т |
| Address | Ádriss | Áдрес |
| Heading | Zagalóvak | Заголо́вок |
| Signature | Pódpiss | По́дпись |
| To write | Pissát | Писа́ть |
| To copy | Snimát kópyu | Снима́ть ко́пию |
| To answer | Atvichát | Отвеча́ть |
| To stick | Zakléyit | Закле́ить |

| To seal | **Zapichátat** | Запеча́тать |
| To send | **Atprávit (passlát)** | Отпра́вить |
| | | (посла́ть) |

There are paper and envelopes on the desk

**Na péessminnam stalyéh yést bumága ee kanvyérty**

На пи́сьменном столе́ есть бума́га и конве́рты

I have to write an urgent letter

**Yá dólzhin napissát sróchnaye peessmóh**

Я до́лжен написа́ть сро́чное письмо́

I am expecting important news

**Yá azhidáyu vázhnaye sa-abshchénye**

Я ожида́ю ва́жное сообще́ние

I have several letters to answer

**Yá dólzhin atvyétit na nyéskalka péessim**

Я до́лжен отве́тить на не́сколько пи́сем

You have not answered my letter

**Vi ni atvyétily na mayóh peessmóh**

Вы не отве́тили на моё письмо́

I explained it all to you in my letter

**Yá vam vsyóh izlazhéel v mayóm pissmyéh**

Я Вам всё изложи́л в моём письме́

My sincere congratulations!

**Mayóh éeskrinnyeye pazdra-vlyénye**

Моё и́скреннее поздравле́ние

Many happy returns of the day!

**Pazdravlyáyu sa dnyóm razhdyénya**

Поздравля́ю со днём рожде́ния

# Leisure Activities

## Wireless and television

| Audibility (reception) | **Slíshimast (priyóm)** | Слы́шимость (приём) |
| Wireless set | **Radiopriyómnik** | Радиоприёмник |
| Television set | **Tiliveézar** | Телеви́зор |
| Loud speaker | **Gromkagavaréetyil** | Громкоговори́тель |
| Battery set | **Priyómnik rabó-tayushchy na batarýéye** | Приёмник рабó-тающий на батарéе |
| Volume | **Palnatáh zvúka** | Полнотá звýка |
| Tuning | **Riguléeravanye** | Регули́рование |
| Aerial | **Antyénna** | Антéнна |
| Direct current | **Pryimóy tok** | Прямóй ток |
| Alternating current | **Pirimýénny tok** | Переме́нный ток |
| Interference | **Radiopamýékhy (tilipamýékhy)** | Радиопомéхи (телепомéхи) |
| Fading | **Zamiránye radio-priyóma (fýéding)** | Замирáние радио-приёма (фéдинг) |
| Long (medium, short) wave | **Dléennaya (sryéd-nyaya, karótkaya) valná** | Дли́нная (срéдняя, корóткая) волнá |
| Gramophone record | **Plastéenka** | Пласти́нка |
| Announcer | **Déektar** | Ди́ктор |
| Listeners | **Radioslúshatyily** | Радиослýшатели |
| Switch on (off) the set | **Fklyuchéet (víklyuchit) rádio (tiliveézar)** | Включи́ть (вы́ключить) рáдио (теле-ви́зор) |
| News | **Paslyédniye izvyéstya** | Послéдние извéстия |
| Weather report (forecast) | **Svódka pagódy (pragnós pagódy)** | Свóдка погóды (прогнóз погóды) |

My set has gone wrong

**Móy priyómnik ispórchin**
Мой приёмник испо́рчен

Can you recommend a good
shop for radio repairs?

**Mózhitye vi rikamindavát
kharóshy magazéen dlyá
rimónta radiopriyómnikaf ?**
Мо́жете вы рекомендова́ть
хоро́ший магази́н для
ремо́нта радиоприёмников?

Can you send somebody to look
at my set?

**Mózhitye vi prislát kavó-nibút
asmatryét priyómnik?**
Мо́жете вы присла́ть кого-
нибу́дь осмотре́ть приёмник?

You need new valves

**Slyéduyit sminéet lámpy**
Сле́дует смени́ть ла́мпы

Do you want to listen to
programme parade?

**Khatéetye praslúshat radio-
pragrámmu?**
Хоти́те прослу́шать радио-
програ́мму?

We'll watch a football match on
television

**Búdyim smatryét tilipiridáchu
futbólnava mátcha**
Бу́дем смотре́ть телепереда́чу
футбо́льного ма́тча

Did you hear (see) the broadcast
of the Philharmonic
Orchestra?

**Vi slúshaly (smatryély) piridáchu
filarmanéechiskava arkyéstra?**
Вы слу́шали (смотре́ли) пере-
да́чу филармони́ческого
орке́стра?

I always listen to the weather
forecast and the news

**Yá vsyegdá slúshayu pragnózy
pagódy ee paslyédniye izvyéstya**
Я всегда́ слу́шаю прогно́зы
пого́ды и после́дние изве́стия

Did you hear the news this
morning?

**Vi slíshaly nóvasty sivódnya
útram?**
Вы слы́шали но́вости сего́дня
у́тром?

What did they say about the
weather?

**Shto skazály a pagódye?**
Что сказа́ли о пого́де?

| There was good (bad) reception today | **Sivódnya bwíl kharóshy (plakhóy) priyóm** |
| | Сегодня был хороший (плохой) приём |
| There is no interference today | **Sivódnya pamyékh nyé bwíla** |
| | Сегодня помех не было |
| The clarity of the picture and the purity of the sound were excellent | **Chótkast izabrazhénya ee cheestatáh zvúka bwíly fpalnyéh kharóshye** |
| | Чёткость изображения и чистота звука были вполне хорошие |

## Photography

| Camera | **Fataapparát (fatagraféechisky apparát)** | Фотоаппарат (фотографический аппарат) |
| Film | **Plyónka** | Плёнка |
| Photograph | **Snéemak (fóto, fatagráfiya)** | Снимок (фото, фотография) |
| Time exposure | **Dléetyilnaya ekspazéetsya** | Длительная экспозиция |
| Exposure | **Vídirzhka** | Выдержка |
| To expose to the light | **Vistavlyát na svyét** | Выставлять на свет |
| Lens | **Abyektéef** | Объектив |
| Light filter | **Svitaféeltr** | Светофильтр |
| Shutter | **Diafrágma** | Диафрагма |
| Colour photography | **Tsvitnáya fatagráfiya** | Цветная фотография |
| A single shot | **Kadr** | Кадр |
| Negative | **Nigatéef** | Негатив |
| Under-exposed | **Nidadyérzhanny** | Недодержанный |
| Over-exposed | **Piridyérzhanny** | Передержанный |
| To develop | **Prayavlyát** | Проявлять |
| To enlarge | **Uviléechivat** | Увеличивать |
| To adjust, adapt | **Prispasablyát** | Приспособлять |

| | |
|---|---|
| Is photography allowed here? | **Mózhna zdyés fatagrafeéeravat?**<br>Мо́жно здесь фотографи́ровать? |
| You must hand in your camera | **Vi dalzhneé zdát vash fata-apparát**<br>Вы должны́ сдать ваш фото-аппара́т |
| Where can I get photographic material? | **Gdyé mózhna dastát fatagrafeé-chiskiye prinadlyézhnasty?**<br>Где мо́жно доста́ть фотогра-фи́ческие принадле́жности? |
| May I have a film? | **Magú yá pulucheét plyónky?**<br>Могу́ я получи́ть плёнку? |
| Could you put it in for me? | **Mózhitye vi yiyóh fstávit?**<br>Мо́жете вы её вста́вить? |
| Do you develop films? | **Prayavlyáyitye vi plyónky?**<br>Проявля́ете вы плёнки? |
| The photos are under-exposed | **Sneémky nidadyérzhany**<br>Сни́мки недоде́ржаны |
| Can you intensify them? | **Mózhna yéekh useélit?**<br>Мо́жно их уси́лить? |
| Could you make prints of these pictures? | **Mózhitye napichátat éty sním̮ky?**<br>Мо́жете напеча́тать э́ти сни́мки? |
| Three copies of each | **Pa tree eksimplyára kázhdava**<br>По три экземпля́ра ка́ждого |
| Have you any photo albums? | **Yést u vass albómy dlyá fatagráfiy?**<br>Есть у вас альбо́мы для фотогра́фий? |
| Do you keep frames? | **Yést u vass rámky?**<br>Есть у вас ра́мки? |
| I want to have my photo taken | **Yá khachú snyátsya**<br>Я хочу́ сня́ться |
| I am going to have my photo taken | **Yá idú snimátsya**<br>Я иду́ снима́ться |

## Winter sports

| To ski | Khadéet na lízhakh | Ходи́ть на лы́жах |
| Skis | Lízhy | Лы́жи |
| Sticks | Pálky | Па́лки |
| Bindings | Rimneé | Ремни́ |
| Ski-wax | Vosk | Воск |
| Sun-glasses | Tyómniye achkeé | Тёмные очки́ |
| Skier | Lízhnik | Лы́жник |
| Beginner | Nachináyushchy | Начина́ющий |
| Ski-ing wear | Lízhny kastyúm | Лы́жный костю́м |
| A turn | Pavarót | Поворо́т |
| Ski jump | Lízhny prizhók | Лы́жный прыжо́к |
| Down-hill run | Byék na lízhakh | Бег на лы́жах |
| Sledge, luge | Sány | Са́ни |
| Bobsleigh | Bóbsley | Бо́бслей |
| Runners | Palózya | Поло́зья |
| Sledge-track (bob-run) | Daróshka dlyá sanyéy (dlyá bóbsley) | Доро́жка для саней (для бо́бслей) |
| Fresh snow | Svyézhy snyék | Све́жий снег |
| Powder snow | Lyókhy snyék | Лёгкий снег |
| Ice | Lyót | Лёд |
| Snow drift | Snyézhny sugróp | Сне́жный сугро́б |
| Avalanche of snow | Snyézhny abvál | Сне́жный обва́л |
| Snow plough | Snyéga-achisteétyil | Снегоочисти́тель |
| Skates | Kankeé | Коньки́ |
| Ice-rink | Katók | Като́к |
| To skate | Katátsya na kankákh | Ката́ться на конька́х |

Can we hire skis here?    **Mózhim mi zdyés vzyát na prakát lízhy?**

Мо́жем мы здесь взять на прока́т лы́жи?

Is there a ski instructor here?    **Yést zdyés lízhny instrúktar?**

Есть здесь лы́жный инстру́ктор?

| | |
|---|---|
| Have you ever done any ski-ing? | **Vi khadéely kudá-nibút na lízhakh?** |
| | Вы ходи́ли когда́-нибудь на лы́жах? |
| No, I'm a beginner | **Nyét, yá nachináyushchy** |
| | Нет, я начина́ющий |
| You must fasten your bindings properly | **Vi dalzhneé priládit rimneé** |
| | Вы должны́ прила́дить ремни́ |
| The snow isn't good for ski-ing today | **Snyék sivódnya ni gadeétsya dlyá lizh** |
| | Снег сего́дня не годи́тся для лыж |
| I don't like the crust on the snow | **Mnyé ni nrávitsya nast na snigú** |
| | Мне не нра́вится наст на снегу́ |
| New snow is very dangerous for beginners | **Svyézhy snyék óchin apássin dlyá nachináyushchikh** |
| | Све́жий снег о́чень опа́сен для начина́ющих |
| Where is the ski jump? | **Gdyé trampleén dlyá lízhnikh prishkóf?** |
| | Где трампли́н для лы́жных прыжко́в? |
| The down-hill run is rather steep | **Spusk pód garu davólna krutóy** |
| | Спуск по́д гору дово́льно круто́й |
| Have you ever done any sledging? | **Vi katálys kagdá-nibút na sánkakh?** |
| | Вы ката́лись когда́-нибудь на са́нках? |
| Shall we go up by the funicular and come down on the bobsleigh? | **Padneémimsya pa górnay zhilyéznay darógye ee spústimsya na bóbsley?** |
| | Подни́мемся по го́рной желе́зной доро́ге и спу́стимся на бо́бслей? |
| Do you like skating? | **Vi lyúbitye katátsya na kankákh?** |
| | Вы лю́бите ката́ться на конька́х? |

| Get your skates and let's go to the rink | **Biréetye kankeé, paydyómtye na katók** |
| | Берите коньки, пойдёмте на каток |
| Will the ice hold? | **Lyót vídirzhit (dastátachna kryépky)?** |
| | Лёд выдержит (достаточно крепкий)? |
| There's going to be an exhibition of figure-skating | **Búdyit pridstavlyénye figúrnava katánya** |
| | Будет представление фигурного катанья |
| You haven't fastened your skates properly | **Vi nikharashóh priládily kankeé** |
| | Вы нехорошо приладили коньки |

## Water sports

| Swimming | **Plávanye** | Плавание |
| To swim | **Plávat** | Плавать |
| Swimming pool | **Bassyéyn dlyá plávanya** | Бассейн для плавания |
| Swimming bath | **Zakríty bassyéyn dlyá plávanya** | Закрытый бассейн для плавания |
| Bathing | **Kupánye** | Купанье |
| To bathe | **Kupátsya** | Купаться |
| Bathing costume | **Kupálny kastyúm** | Купальный костюм |
| Bathing trunks | **Kupálniye trúsiky** | Купальные трусики |
| Bathing towel | **Kupálnaye palatyéntsa** | Купальное полотенце |
| Bathing cap | **Kupálny shlyém** | Купальный шлем |
| Diving board | **Trampleén dlyá niryánya** | Трамплин для ныряния |
| To dive | **Niryát** | Нырять |
| To drown | **Tanút** | Тонуть |

Shall we go bathing?

**Khateetye kupátsya?**
Хоти́те купа́ться?

Can we swim in the river?

**Mózhna plávat v rikyéh?**
Мо́жно пла́вать в реке́?

No, you must go to the swimming pool

**Nyét, vi dalzhnee paytee v bassyéyn dlyá plávanya**
Нет, вы должны́ пойти́ в бассе́йн для пла́вания

No bathing!

**Zdyés kupátsya zaprisháyitsya!**
Здесь купа́ться запреща́ется!

Are you a good swimmer?

**Vi kharashóh plávayitye?**
Вы хорошо́ пла́ваете?

Let's swim to the opposite bank

**Paplivyóm k drugómu byérigu**
Поплывём к друго́му бе́регу

The current is too strong

**Tichénye sleeshkam seelnaye**
Тече́ние сли́шком си́льное

Can you swim on your back?

**Umyéyitye vi plávat na spinyéh?**
Уме́ете вы пла́вать на спине́?

He is floating

**On dyérzhitsya na pavyérkhnasty vadíy**
Он де́ржится на пове́рхности воды́

I've got cramp in my right calf

**U minyá súdaraga f právay ikryéh**
У меня́ су́дорога в пра́вой икре́

Swim and help him, he's drowning

**Pliveetye k nimú ee pamageetye yimú, on tónit**
Плыви́те к нему́ и помоги́те ему́, он то́нет

He was nearly drowned

**On pachtee utanúl**
Он почти́ утону́л

Hang on to the life line

**Dirzhéetyes za spassátilnuyu viryófku**
Держи́тесь за спаса́тельную верёвку

Stay in shallow water

**Astaváytyes tam, gdyé myélka**
Остава́йтесь там, где ме́лко

| Don't swim beyond the danger-post | **Ni plávaytye dálshey stalbá**<br>Не плавайте дальше столба |
| Only strong swimmers are allowed in the pool | **Tólka kharóshiye plavtsíy dapuskáyutsya v bassyéyn**<br>Только хорошие пловцы допускаются в бассейн |
| Can you recommend a good seaside resort? | **Mózhitye vi rikamindavát kharóshy marskóy kurórt?**<br>Можете вы рекомендовать хороший морской курорт? |
| I want to spend my holiday by the sea | **Yá khachú pravistée ótpusk ókala mórya**<br>Я хочу провести отпуск около моря |

## Rowing and boating

| Boat | **Lótka** | Лодка |
|------|-----------|-------|
| Rowing boat | **Visyélnaya lótka** | Весельная лодка |
| Canoe | **Chilnók** | Челнок |
| Collapsible boat | **Skladnáya lótka** | Складная лодка |
| Racing boat | **Gónachnaya lótka** | Гоночная лодка |
| Boat-race | **Lódachniye gónky** | Лодочные гонки |
| Starboard | **Právy bort** | Правый борт |
| Port | **Lyévy bort** | Левый борт |
| Oar | **Visslóh** | Весло |
| Rudder | **Rul** | Руль |
| Pole | **Shest** | Шест |
| To row | **Gristée** | Грести |
| To steer | **Upravlyát** | Управлять |

| Boats for hire | **Zdayútsya lótky na prakát**<br>Сдаются лодки на прокат |
| Come to the jetty | **Prikhadéetye k mólu**<br>Приходите к молу |
| The boat has sprung a leak | **Lótka daláh tyéch**<br>Лодка дала течь |

Let's go and watch the Boat Race — **Paydyómtye smatryét lódachniye gónky**

Пойдёмте смотре́ть ло́дочные го́нки

## Football

| Game | **Igráh** | Игра́ |
|---|---|---|
| Match | **Match** | Матч |
| Ball | **Myách** | Мяч |
| Team | **Kamánda** | Кома́нда |
| Player | **Igrók** | Игро́к |
| Goal-keeper | **Vratár** | Врата́рь |
| Full-back | **Zashchéetnik** | Защи́тник |
| Half-back | **Paluzashchéetnik** | Полузащи́тник |
| Defence | **Zashchéeta** | Защи́та |
| Forward | **Napadáyushchy** | Напада́ющий |
| Attack; forward line | **Napadyénye** | Нападе́ние |
| Referee | **Sudyáh** | Судья́ |
| Goal-posts | **Varóta** | Воро́та |
| A goal | **Gol** | Гол |
| To score a goal | **Zabéet gol** | Заби́ть гол |
| A shot | **Udár** | Уда́р |
| To kick | **Udaryát (nagóy)** | Ударя́ть (ного́й) |
| To beat | **Pabizhdát** | Побежда́ть |

Shall we go and watch the game between Leningrad and Moscow? — **Ni paytée ly nam pasmatryét na futbólny match myézhdu Liningrádam ee Maskvóy?**

Не пойти́ ли нам посмотре́ть на футбо́льный матч ме́жду Ленингра́дом и Москво́й?

Are these teams famous? — **Znaminéety éty kamándy?**

Знамени́ты э́ти кома́нды?

What a wonderful shot! — **Kakóy zamichátilny udár!**

Како́й замеча́тельный уда́р!

| | | |
|---|---|---|
| The goal is well defended | **U varót kharóshaya zashchéeta** | |
| | У воро́т хоро́шая защи́та | |
| What's the score? | **Kakóy shchot?** | |
| | Како́й счёт? | |
| In the first half the score was in our favour | **F pyérvay palavéenye shchot bwil f náshu pólzu** | |
| | В пе́рвой полови́не счёт был в на́шу по́льзу | |
| How many goals did they score? | **Skólka anée zabéely galóf?** | |
| | Ско́лько они́ заби́ли голо́в? | |
| Leningrad won 3–1 | **Liningrátsy víyigraly tree-adéen** | |
| | Ленингра́дцы вы́играли три-оди́н | |

# Gymnastics and athletics

| | | |
|---|---|---|
| Gymnasium | **Gimnastéechisky zal** | Гимнасти́ческий зал |
| Apparatus | **Apparatúra dlyá gimnástiky** | Аппарату́ра для гимна́стики |
| Parallel bars | **Parallyélniye brússya** | Паралле́льные бру́сья |
| Rope | **Kanát** | Кана́т |
| To climb | **Lázit** | Ла́зить |
| Horse | **Kózly** | Ко́злы |
| Pole | **Shest** | Шест |
| Spring-board | **Trampléen** | Трампли́н |
| To jump | **Prígat** | Пры́гать |
| Cinder track | **Tryék** | Трек |
| To run, to race | **Bizhát, sastyizátsya** | Бежа́ть, состяза́ться |
| A race | **Gónky** | Го́нки |
| Relay race | **Gónky s estafyétay** | Го́нки с эстафе́той |
| Finish, 'tape' | **Féenish** | Фи́ниш |
| High (long) jump | **Prizhók v vissatú (na rastayánye)** | Прыжо́к в высоту́ (на расстоя́ние) |

| Vest | **Máyka** | Ма́йка |
| Shorts | **Trúsiky** | Тру́сики |
| Gym shoes | **Túfly dlyá** | Ту́фли для |
| | **gimnástiky** | гимна́стики |

Do you do exercises in the morning?

**Dyélayitye vi pa utrám gimnástiku?**

Де́лаете вы по утра́м гимна́стику?

Are you entering for the thousand metres?

**Sastyizáyityes vi v gónkakh na tíssyichu myétraf ?**

Состяза́етесь вы в го́нках на ты́сячу ме́тров?

Who broke the record for the high jump?

**Kto pabéel rikórd na prizhók v vissatú?**

Кто поби́л реко́рд на прыжо́к в высоту́?

Shall we go and watch the javelin and the discus?

**Ni paytée ly nam pasmatryét na mitánye kapyáh ee déeska?**

Не пойти́ ли нам посмотре́ть на мета́нье копья́ и ди́ска?

# Reference Section

## Time

| | | |
|---|---|---|
| Clock, watch | **Chassíy** | Часы́ |
| Wrist watch | **Ruchnéeye chassíy** | Ручны́е часы́ |
| Alarm clock | **Budéelnik** | Буди́льник |
| Watchmaker | **Chassafshchéek** | Часовщи́к |
| To repair | **Chinéet** | Чини́ть |
| To be fast (lose) | **Ittée fpiryót (atstavát)** | Идти́ вперёд (отстава́ть) |
| To set right | **Pastavít** | Поста́вить |
| To get up | **Fstavát** | Встава́ть |
| To go to bed | **Lazhéetsya spat** | Ложи́ться спать |
| Early | **Rána** | Ра́но |
| Late | **Pózdna** | По́здно |
| Punctually, on time | **Vó-vremya** | Во́-время |
| Morning | **Útra** | У́тро |
| Afternoon (day) | **Dyén** | День |
| Evening | **Vyéchir** | Ве́чер |
| Night | **Noch** | Ночь |
| Midday | **Póldyin** | По́лдень |
| Midnight | **Pólnach** | По́лночь |
| In the morning | **Útram** | У́тром |
| In the afternoon | **Dnyóm** | Днём |
| In the evening | **Vyéchiram** | Ве́чером |
| At night | **Nóchyu** | Но́чью |
| At noon (midnight) | **F póldyin (f pólnach)** | В по́лдень (в по́лночь) |
| Yesterday | **Fchiráh** | Вчера́ |
| Today | **Sivódnya** | Сего́дня |
| Tomorrow | **Záftra** | За́втра |
| The day before yesterday | **Pazafchiráh (tryétyiva dnyá)** | Позавчера́ (тре́тьего дня) |
| The day after tomorrow | **Poslizáftra** | Послеза́втра |

| | | |
|---|---|---|
| Yesterday morning (afternoon, evening, night) | **Fchiráh útram (dnyóm, vyé-chiram, nóchyu)** | Вчерá ýтром (днём, вéчером, нóчью) |
| This morning (afternoon, evening, night) | **Sivódnya útram (dnyóm, vyé-chiram, nóchyu)** | Сегóдня ýтром (днём, вéчером, нóчью) |
| Tomorrow morning (afternoon, evening, night) | **Záftra útram (dnyóm, vyé-chiram, nóchyu)** | Зáвтра ýтром (днём, вéчером, нóчью) |
| Week | **Nidyélya** | Недéля |
| This (last, next) week | **Na étay (próshlay, búdushye) nidyélye** | На э́той (прóшлой, бýдушье) недéле |
| The days of the week | **Dnée nidyélee** | Дни недéли |
| Sunday | **Vaskrissyénye** | Воскресéнье |
| Monday | **Panidyélnik** | Понедéльник |
| Tuesday | **Ftórnik** | Втóрник |
| Wednesday | **Sridáh** | Средá |
| Thursday | **Chitvyérk** | Четвéрг |
| Friday | **Pyátnitsa** | Пя́тница |
| Saturday | **Subbóta** | Суббóта |
| On Monday, on Thursday, on Tuesday, on Sunday, on Wednesday, on Friday, on Saturday | **F panidyélnik, f chitvyérk, vo ftórnik, v vaskrissyénye, f sryédu, f pyátnitsu, f subbótu** | В понедéльник, в четвéрг, во втóрник, в воскресéнье, в срéду, в пя́тницу, в суббóту |
| The date | **Chisslóh** | Числó |
| Month | **Myéssyits** | Мéсяц |
| Year | **Got** | Год |
| This (last, next) year | **V étam (próshlam, búdushchim) gadú** | В э́том (прóшлом, бýдушем) годý |
| January | **Yinvár** | Янвáрь |
| February | **Fivrál** | Феврáль |
| March | **Mart** | Март |
| April | **Apryél** | Апрéль |
| May | **Máy** | Май |
| June | **Eeún** | Ию́нь |

| July | **Eeúl** | Июль |
| August | **Ávgust** | Áвгуст |
| September | **Sintyábr** | Сентя́брь |
| October | **Aktyábr** | Октя́брь |
| November | **Nayábr** | Ноя́брь |
| December | **Dikábr** | Дека́брь |
| In January | **V yinvaryéh** | В январе́ |
| In July | **V eeúlye** | В ию́ле |
| Spring | **Vissnáh** | Весна́ |
| Summer | **Lyéta** | Ле́то |
| Autumn | **Óssyin** | Óсень |
| Winter | **Zeemáh** | Зима́ |
| In spring (in summer, in autumn, in winter) | **Vissnóy (lyétam, óssyinyu, zeemóy)** | Весно́й (ле́том, óсенью, зимо́й) |
| Public holiday | **Prázdnik** | Пра́здник |
| Christmas | **Razhdistvóh** | Рождество́ |
| Easter | **Pásskha** | Па́сха |
| Whitsun | **Tróyitsin dyén** | Тро́ицын день |
| 1 May (International Labour Day) | **Pyérvaye máya (Prázdnik mizhdu-naródnay salidárnasty pralitiryáta)** | Пе́рвое ма́я (Пра́здник междунаро́дной солида́рности пролетариа́та) |
| 7 Nov. (Anniversary of the October Revolution) | **Sidmóye nayabryáh (gadafshchéena Aktyábr-skay Rivalyútsee)** | Седьмо́е ноября́ (годовщи́на Октя́брьской Револю́ции) |
| 23 Feb. (Red Army Day) | **Dvátsat tryétye fivralyáh (dyén Krásnay Ármee)** | Два́дцать тре́тье февраля́ (день Кра́сной Áрмии) |
| A second | **Sikúnda** | Секу́нда |
| A minute | **Minúta** | Мину́та |
| An hour | **Chass** | Час |
| A day | **Dyén** | День |
| A twenty-four-hour period | **Sútky** | Су́тки |

| When? | **Kagdá?** | Когда́? |
| Now | **Tipyér** | Тепе́рь |
| Right now; this minute | **Sicháss** | Сейча́с |
| Then (at that time) | **Tagdá** | Тогда́ |
| A long time; long since | **Davnóh** | Давно́ |
| Recently; not long ago | **Nidávna** | Неда́вно |
| The other day; recently | **Na dnyákh** | На дня́х |
| Ago | **Tamú nasát** | Тому́ наза́д |
| In half an hour (two days, a week, a month, a year, several years) | **Chériz palchassáh (dva dnyá, nidyélyu, myéssyits, got, nyéskalka lyét)** | Че́рез полчаса́ (два дня, неде́лю, ме́сяц, год, не́сколько лет) |
| Per day (week, month) | **V dyén (nidyélyu, myéssyits)** | В день (неде́лю, ме́сяц) |

We are going to the theatre this evening

**Sivódnya vyéchiram mi idyóm f tiátr**

Сего́дня ве́чером мы идём в теа́тр

Tomorrow we are going to Pushkino for the whole day

**Záftra mi yédyem f Púshkina na vyés dyén**

За́втра мы е́дем в Пу́шкино на весь день

I got back the day before yesterday

**Yá virnúlsya pazafchiráh (tryétyiva dnyá)**

Я верну́лся позавчера́ (тре́тьего дня)

I am leaving again tomorrow (the day after tomorrow, next week)

**Yá uyezháyu apyát záftra (poslizáftra, na búdushchey nidyélye)**

Я уезжа́ю опя́ть за́втра (послеза́втра, на бу́дущей неде́ле)

There will be a concert next week

**Na búdushchey nidyélye búdyit kantsért**

На бу́дущей неде́ле бу́дет конце́рт

I shall be back in a week's time

**Yá virnúss chériz nidyélyu**

Я верну́сь че́рез неде́лю

Two weeks ago I was in London

**Dve nidyély tamú nazát yá bwíl f Lóndanye**

Две неде́ли тому́ наза́д я был в Ло́ндоне

In two days' (a week's) time I shall be in Moscow

**Chériz dva dnyá (nidyélyu) yá búdu f Maskvyéh**

Че́рез два дня (неде́лю) я бу́ду в Москве́

On Saturday I shall be busy all day

**F súbbotu yá búdu zányit(a) vyés dyén**

В суббо́ту я бу́ду за́нят(а́) весь день

What did you do last Sunday?

**Shto vi dyélaly f próshlaye vaskrissyénye?**

Что вы де́лали в про́шлое воскресе́нье?

I am leaving next Monday

**Yá uyezháyu v búdushchy panidyélnik**

Я уезжа́ю в бу́дущий понеде́льник

What date is it today?

**Kakóye sivódnya chisslóh?**

Како́е сего́дня число́?

Today is 15 Sept.

**Sivódnya pitnátsataye sintibryáh**

Сего́дня пятна́дцатое сентября́

We have tickets for 9 Aug.

**Y nass bilyéty na divyátaye ávgusta**

У нас биле́ты на девя́тое а́вгуста

On what date were you born?

**Kakóva chissláh vi radeélis?**

Како́го числа́ вы роди́лись?

| | |
|---|---|
| My birthday is on 10 Oct. | **Mayóh razhdyénye dissyátava aktibryáh**<br>Моё рождéние деся́того октября́ |
| In what year were you born? | **F kakóm gadú vi radéelis?**<br>В како́м году́ вы роди́лись? |
| In 1945 | **F tíssyicha divyitsót sórak pyátam gadú**<br>В ты́сяча девятьсо́т со́рок пя́том году́ |
| What time is it? | **Katóry chass?**<br>Кото́рый час? |
| Eight o'clock | **Vóssyim chassóf**<br>Во́семь часо́в |
| Five past eight | **Pyát minút divyátava**<br>Пять мину́т девя́того |
| A quarter past eight | **Chétvirt divyátava**<br>Че́тверть девя́того |
| Half past eight | **Palavéena divyátava**<br>Полови́на девя́того |
| A quarter to nine | **Biz chétvirty dyévyit**<br>Без че́тверти де́вять |
| 8.0 a.m. | **Vóssyim chassóf utráh**<br>Во́семь часо́в утра́ |
| 8.0 p.m. | **Vóssyim chassóf vyéchira**<br>Во́семь часо́в ве́чера |
| 1.0 p.m. (1.0 a.m.) | **Chass dnyá (chass nóchy)**<br>Час дня (час но́чи) |
| About four o'clock | **Ókala chitiryókh chassóf**<br>О́коло четырёх часо́в |
| A little later | **Nimnóga pazdnyéye**<br>Немно́го поздне́е |
| At what time? | **F katóram chassú?**<br>В кото́ром часу́? |
| He arrived at 1.0 a.m. (at 2.0 p.m.) | **On priyékhal f chass nóchy (v dva chassáh dnyá)**<br>Он прие́хал в час но́чи (в два часа́ дня) |

| | |
|---|---|
| We shall expect you at exactly five o'clock | **Mi zhdyóm vass róvna f pyát chassóf**<br>Мы ждём вас ро́вно в пять часо́в |
| Come at half past four | **Prikhadeétye f palaveénye pyátava (f palpyátava)**<br>Приходи́те в полови́не п'я́того (в полпя́того) |
| Come at a quarter to five | **Prikhadeétye biz chétvirty pyát**<br>Приходи́те без че́тверти пять |
| The train leaves (arrives) at 2.30 | **Póyezd atkhódit (prikhódit) v dva treétsat**<br>По́езд отхо́дит (прихо́дит) в два три́дцать |
| You must be at the station half an hour before the train goes | **Vi dalzhneé bwít na vakzálye za palchassáh do atkhóda póyezda**<br>Вы должны́ быть на вокза́ле за полчаса́ до отхо́да по́езда |
| Five minutes before the train arrives | **Za pyát minút do prikhóda póyezda**<br>За пять мину́т до прихо́да по́езда |
| The box-office is open from 10.0 a.m. to 8.0 p.m. | **Kássa atkríta ot dissyiteé utráh do vóssmee vyéchira**<br>Ка́сса откры́та от десяти́ утра́ до восьми́ ве́чера |
| Hurry up, it's half past seven now | **Skaryéye (tarapeétyes) sicháss palaveéna vassmóva**<br>Скоре́й (торопи́тесь), сейча́с полови́на восьмо́го |
| Don't be late! | **Ni apázdivaytye!**<br>Не опа́здывайте! |
| Don't turn up at the very last moment! | **Ni yavlyáytyes f paslyédnyuyu minútu!**<br>Не явля́йтесь в после́днюю мину́ту! |

| | |
|---|---|
| I shall arrive in time | **Yá pridú (priyédu) vóvremya**<br>Я приду́ (прие́ду) во́-время |
| It's time to go | **Paráh ittée (yékhat)**<br>Пора́ идти́ (е́хать) |
| It's time to get up (go to bed) | **Paráh fstavát (lazheetsya spat)**<br>Пора́ встава́ть (ложи́ться спать) |
| We shall be late | **Mi apazdáyem**<br>Мы опозда́ем |
| You are extremely late | **Vi séelna apazdály**<br>Вы си́льно опозда́ли |
| I've been waiting for you for a long time | **Ya vass davnóh zhdú**<br>Я вас давно́ жду |
| He left a long time ago | **On davnóh uyékhal**<br>Он давно́ уе́хал |
| How late were you? | **Na skólka vi apazdály?**<br>На ско́лько вы опозда́ли? |
| Almost an hour | **Pachtée na chass**<br>Почти́ на час |
| They missed that train by a minute | **Anée apazdály na état póyezd na adnú minútu**<br>Они́ опозда́ли на э́тот по́езд на одну́ мину́ту |
| Can you spare me a moment? | **Magú yá vass zadirzhát na minútu?**<br>Могу́ я вас заде́ржать на мину́ту? |
| I haven't time | **U minyá nyét vryéminy**<br>У меня́ нет вре́мени |
| Just a moment, please (wait a moment) | **Adnú minútu, pazhálusta (padazhdéetye minútu)!**<br>Одну́ мину́ту, пожа́луйста (подожди́те мину́ту)! |
| Can you tell me what time it is? | **Mózhtye skazát mnyé katóry chass?**<br>Мо́жете сказа́ть мне кото́рый час? |

Is your watch right?

**Váshy chassée idút vyérna?**
Ва́ши часы́ иду́т ве́рно?

It always keeps good time

**Anée vsyegdá idút vyérna**
Они́ всегда́ иду́т ве́рно

It's ten minutes fast

**Anée na dyéssyit minút fpiryót**
Они́ на де́сять мину́т вперёд

It's a quarter of an hour slow

**Anée atstayút na chétvirt chasáh**
Они́ отстаю́т на че́тверть часа́

Set your watch by the station
  clock

**Pastáftye svayée chassíy pa
  vakzálnim**
Поста́вьте свои́ часы́ по
  вокза́льным

My watch has stopped

**Mayée chassíy astanavéelis**
Мои́ часы́ останови́лись

I must have my watch repaired

**Yá dólzhin atdát mayée chassíy
  f pachéenku**
Я до́лжен отда́ть мои́ часы́
  в почи́нку

How frequently do you get
  foreign papers?

**Kak chásta vi palucháyitye
  zarubyézhniye gazyéty?**
Как ча́сто получа́ете вы
  зарубе́жные газе́ты?

Every day

**Kázhdy dyén**
Ка́ждый день

Twice a week

**Dva ráza f nidyélyu**
Два ра́за в неде́лю

At dawn

**Na rassvyétye**
На рассве́те

At dusk

**F súmirky**
В су́мерки

It gets dark very early

**Óchin rána timnyéyit**
О́чень ра́но темне́ет

# Weather

| | | |
|---|---|---|
| Weather | **Pagóda** | Погóда |
| Air | **Vózdukh** | Вóздух |
| Heat | **Zharáh** | Жарá |
| Cold | **Khólat** | Хóлод |
| Rain | **Dózhd** | Дождь |
| Dew | **Rasságh** | Росá |
| Snow | **Snyék** | Снег |
| Frost | **Marós** | Морóз |
| Fog | **Tumán** | Тумáн |
| Ice | **Lyót** | Лёд |
| Hail | **Grat** | Град |
| Sky | **Nyéba** | Нéбо |

| | | |
|---|---|---|
| Sunshine (there was, will be sunshine) | **Sóntseh (bwíla, búdyit sóntseh)** | Сóлнце (бы́ло, бу́дет сóлнце) |
| Light cloud | **Óblako** | Óблако |
| Storm cloud | **Túcha** | Ту́ча |
| Wind | **Vyétir** | Вéтер |
| Snowstorm; blizzard | **Mityél** | Метéль |
| Thunderstorm | **Grazáh** | Грозá |
| Thunder | **Grom** | Гром |
| Lightning | **Mólnya** | Мóлния |
| It is cold | **Khóladna** | Хóлодно |
| It is warm | **Tiplóh** | Теплó |
| It is hot | **Zhárka** | Жáрко |
| It is clear | **Yássna** | Ясно |
| It is (was, will be) raining | **Idyót (bwil búdyit) dózhd** | Идёт (был, бу́дет) дождь |
| It is (was, will be) snowing | **Idyót (bwíl, búdyit) snyék** | Идёт (был, бу́дет) снег |
| It is freezing | **Marózit** | Морóзит |

| | |
|---|---|
| What is the weather like? | **Kakáya pagóda?** |
| | Какáя погóда? |
| The weather is fine (bad) | **Kharóshaya (plakháya) pagóda** |
| | Хорóшая (плохáя) погóда |

| | |
|---|---|
| It's a beautiful day | **Prikrásny dyén**<br>Прекрасный день |
| The weather is beautiful (dull) | **Pagóda prikrásnaya (pásmurnaya)**<br>Погода прекрасная<br>(пасмурная) |
| The weather is changeable | **Pagóda pirimyénchivaya**<br>Погода переменчивая |
| The weather is settled | **Pagóda ustanavéelis**<br>Погода установилась |
| It's very oppressive | **Óchin dúshna**<br>Очень душно |
| Is it going to thunder? | **Búdyit grazáh?**<br>Будет гроза? |
| Do you think the weather will stay fine? | **Vi dúmayitye, shto pagóda prodyérzhitsya kharóshey?**<br>Вы думаете, что погода продержится хорошей? |
| The wind is cold | **Vyétir khalódny**<br>Ветер холодный |
| There's a gale | **Séelny vyétir**<br>Сильный ветер |
| The wind has dropped | **Vyétir stéekh**<br>Ветер стих |
| The sky is clear | **Nyéba yásnaya**<br>Небо ясное |
| The sky is overcast | **Nyéba zavalaklóh**<br>Небо заволокло |
| It's raining cats and dogs | **Dozhd lyót kak eez vidráh**<br>Дождь льёт как из ведра |
| It's pouring down | **Idyót pralivnóy dozhd**<br>Идёт проливной дождь |
| It's thundering and lightning | **Griméet grom ee svirkáyit mólnya**<br>Гремит гром и сверкает молния |
| I'm wet through | **Yá pramók naskvós**<br>Я промок насквозь |
| Take your raincoat with you | **Vazméetye s sabóy plashch**<br>Возьмите с собой плащ |

| | |
|---|---|
| It's getting cold | **Stanóvitsya khóladna**<br>Стано́вится хо́лодно |
| Do you feel cold? | **Vam khóladna?**<br>Вам хо́лодно? |
| I am quite warm | **Mnyé savsyém tiplóh**<br>Мне совсе́м тепло́ |
| I'm boiling | **Mnyé zhárka**<br>Мне жа́рко |
| It's too sunny here | **Zdyés sléeshkam séelnaye**<br>**sóntseh**<br>Здесь сли́шком си́льное со́лнце |
| Let's sit in the shade | **Syádyimtye f tinée**<br>Ся́демте в тени́ |
| I can't stand the heat | **Yá ni pirinashú zharíy**<br>Я не переношу́ жары́ |
| I am perspiring (delicate) | **Yá vyés v ispárinye**<br>Я весь в испа́рине |
| What does the thermometer read? | **Skólka grádusaf pakázivayit tirmómitr?**<br>Ско́лько гра́дусов пока́зывает термо́метр? |
| The temperature has gone up to 22° Centigrade (=72° Fahrenheit) | **Timpiratúra padnyiláss do dvatsatée dvukh grádusaf**<br>Температу́ра подняла́сь до двадцати́ двух гра́дусов |
| The temperature has fallen by 10 degrees | **Timpiratúra upála na dyéssyit grádusaf**<br>Температу́ра упа́ла на де́сять гра́дусов |
| Ten degrees of frost (−10°C = 14°F) | **Dyéssyit grádusaf maróza**<br>Де́сять гра́дусов моро́за |
| It's freezing hard | **Séelna marózit**<br>Си́льно моро́зит |
| It's very slippery, be careful | **Óchin skólzka, búdtye astarózhny**<br>О́чень ско́льзко, бу́дьте осторо́жны |
| Is it thawing? | **Táyit?**<br>Та́ет? |

# Numerals

*Cardinals*

| Nought | Nol | Ноль |
|---|---|---|
| One | Adéen (adnáh, adnóh) | Оди́н (одна́, одно́) |
| Two | Dva (dvyé) | Два (две) |
| Three | Tree | Три |
| Four | Chitírye | Четы́ре |
| Five | Pyát | Пять |
| Six | Shest | Шесть |
| Seven | Syém | Семь |
| Eight | Vóssyim | Во́семь |
| Nine | Dyévyit | Де́вять |
| Ten | Dyéssyit | Де́сять |
| Eleven | Adéenatsat | Оди́ннадцать |
| Twelve | Dvinátsat | Двена́дцать |
| Thirteen | Trinátsat | Трина́дцать |
| Fourteen | Chitírnatsat | Четы́рнадцать |
| Fifteen | Pitnátsat | Пятна́дцать |
| Sixteen | Shistnátsat | Шестна́дцать |
| Seventeen | Simnátsat | Семна́дцать |
| Eighteen | Vassimnátsat | Восемна́дцать |
| Nineteen | Divyitnátsat | Девятна́дцать |
| Twenty | Dvátsat | Два́дцать |
| Twenty-one | Dvátsat adéen (adnáh, adnóh) | Два́дцать оди́н (одна́, одно́) |
| Twenty-two, etc. | Dvátsat dva (dvyé) | Два́дцать два (две) и т. д. |
| Thirty | Tréetsat | Три́дцать |
| Thirty-one | Tréetsat adéen (adnáh, adnóh) | Три́дцать оди́н (одна́, одно́) |
| Thirty-two, etc. | Tréetsat dva (dvyé) | Три́дцать два (две) и т. д. |
| Forty | Sórak | Со́рок |
| Fifty | Pyitdissyát | Пятьдеся́т |
| Sixty | Shizdissyát | Шестьдеся́т |
| Seventy | Syémdissyat | Се́мьдесят |

| Eighty | **Vóssimdissyat** | Во́семьдесят |
| Ninety | **Divyinósta** | Девяно́сто |
| A hundred | **Stóh** | Сто |
| A hundred and thirty-one | **Stoh tréetsat adéen** | Сто три́дцать оди́н |
| Two hundred | **Dvyésty** | Две́сти |
| Three hundred | **Tréesta** | Три́ста |
| Four hundred | **Chitírista** | Четы́реста |
| Five hundred | **Pyitsót** | Пятьсо́т |
| Six hundred | **Shisót** | Шестьсо́т |
| Seven hundred | **Syimsót** | Семьсо́т |
| Eight hundred | **Vassimsót** | Восемьсо́т |
| Nine hundred | **Divyitsót** | Девятьсо́т |
| A thousand | **Tíssyicha** | Ты́сяча |
| A thousand, four hundred and thirty-six | **Tíssyicha chitíyrista tréetsat shest** | Ты́сяча четы́реста три́дцать шесть |
| Two thousand | **Dvyé tíssyichy** | Две ты́сячи |
| Five thousand | **Pyát tíssyich** | Пять ты́сяч |
| A million | **Millión** | Миллио́н |

*Fractions*

| A half | **Palavéena** | Полови́на |
| A quarter | **Chétvirt** | Че́тверть |
| Three-quarters | **Tree chétvirty** | Три че́тверти |
| A third | **Tryét** | Треть |
| Two-thirds | **Dvyé tryéty** | Две тре́ти |
| One and a half | **Paltaráh, paltaríy** | Полтора́, полторы́ |
| One-fifth (part) | **Adnáh pyátaya (chast)** | Одна́ пя́тая (часть) |
| One-twentieth | **Adnáh dvatsátaya (chast)** | Одна́ двадца́тая |
| One-hundreth | **Adnáh sótaya** | Одна́ со́тая |
| Two-fifths, etc | **Dvyé pyátikh** | Две па́тых и т. д. |
| Two hundredths, etc. | **Dvyé sótikh** | Две со́тых и т. д. |
| Two and a quarter | **Dva s chétvirtyu** | Два с че́твертью |
| Three and a half | **Tree s palavéenay** | Три с полови́ной |

| | | |
|---|---|---|
| Five and three-quarters | **Pyát ee tree chétvirty** | Пять и три че́тверти |
| Ten and seven-eighths | **Dyéssyit ee syém vassmíkh** | Де́сять и семь восьмы́х |
| Nought point three (0·3) | **Nol tsélikh tree dissyátikh** | Ноль це́лых три деся́тых (0,3) |

*Miscellaneous terms*

| | | |
|---|---|---|
| A pair | **Pára** | Па́ра |
| A ten (of something) | **Dissyátak** | Деся́ток |
| A dozen | **Dyúzhina** | Дю́жина |
| A hundred | **Sótnya** | Со́тня |
| Half an hour | **Palchassáh** | Полчаса́ |
| Half a day | **Paldnyáh** | Полдня́ |
| Half a year | **Palgóda** | Полго́да |
| Half a pound (weight) | **Palfúnta** | Полфу́нта |
| Half-bottle | **Palbutíylky** | Полбуты́лки |
| Half a dozen | **Paldyúzhiny** | Полдю́жины |
| How many times? | **Skólka ras?** | Ско́лько раз? |
| Once | **Adéen ras** | (Оди́н) раз |
| Twice | **Dva ráza (dvázhdy)** | Два ра́за (два́жды) |
| Three times | **Tree ráza (tréezhdy)** | Три ра́за (три́жды) |
| Four times | **Chitírye ráza** | Четы́ре ра́за |
| Five (several, many) times | **Pyát (nyéskolka, mnóga) ras** | Пять (не́сколько, мно́го) раз |
| A figure, digit | **Tsíffra** | Ци́фра |
| A number | **Chisslóh** | Число́ |
| Calculation, counting, score | **Shchót** | Счёт |
| To count | **Shchitát** (*perf.* **sashchitát**) | Счита́ть (*perf.* сосчита́ть) |
| Per cent; interest | **Pratsént** | Проце́нт |
| I had ten days' holiday | **U minyá bwíla dyéssyit dnyéy ótpuska** | У меня́ бы́ло де́сять дней о́тпуска |

| | |
|---|---|
| The baby is two years old | **Ribyónku dva góda**<br>Ребёнку два гóда |
| My seat is no. 106 | **Mayóh myésta nómir stoh shest**<br>Моё мéсто нóмер сто шесть |
| He stayed abroad three and a<br>half years | **On próbwil zagranéetsey tree<br>s palavéenay góda**<br>Он прóбыл заграни́цей три<br>с полови́ной гóда |
| I takes about an hour and a half<br>to get there | **Tudá yékhat priblizéetilna<br>paltaráh chassáh**<br>Туда́ éхать приблизи́тельно<br>полтора́ часа́ |
| I spent eighteen months in<br>Sweden | **Yá pravyól paltaráh góda<br>f Shvyétsy**<br>Я провёл полтóра гóда<br>в Швéции |
| I have been waiting half an hour<br>(ten minutes, three quarters of<br>an hour) | **Yá zhdu uzhéh palchassáh<br>(dyéssyit minút, tree chétvirty<br>chassáh)**<br>Я жду ужé полчаса́ (дéсять<br>мину́т, три чéтверти часа́) |
| She stayed away half a day | **Anáh atsútsvavala paldnyáh**<br>Онá отсу́тствовала пóлдня |
| Ten per cent discount for<br>students | **Dlyá studyéntaf skéedka –<br>dyéssyit pratséntaf**<br>Для студéнтов ски́дка – дéсять<br>процéнтов |
| I paid fifty per cent duty | **Yá zaplatéel póshlinu f pitdissyát<br>pratséntaf**<br>Я заплати́л пóшлину в пять-<br>деся́т процéнтов |
| Three per cent tax | **Nalók – tree pratsénta**<br>Налóг – три процéнта |
| He bought half a dozen hand-<br>kerchiefs and a pair of socks | **On kupéel paldyúzhiny platkóf<br>ee páru naskóf**<br>Он купи́л полдю́жины платкóв<br>и пáру носкóв |

| I shall buy her two pairs of nylon stockings | **Yá kuplyú yéy dvyé páry naylónavikh chulkóf** |
| | Я куплю́ ей две па́ры найло́новых чулко́в |
| More than seventy thousand people visited the museum | **Muzyéy pasiteéela bóliye siméedissyity tíssyich chilavyék** |
| | Музе́й посети́ло бо́лее семи́десяти ты́сяч челове́к |
| Count how much money there is here | **Sashchitáytye skólka tut dyénig** |
| | Сосчита́йте ско́лько тут де́нег |
| One rouble (pound, dollar, cent) | **Adéen rubl (funt, dóllar, tsent)** |
| | Оди́н рубль (фунт, до́ллар, цент) |
| Twenty-one roubles, etc. | **Dvátsat adéen rubl** |
| | Два́дцать оди́н рубль и т. д. |
| One kopeck | **Adnáh kapyéyka** |
| | Одна́ копе́йка |
| Two (1½, 3, 4) roubles (pounds, dollars, cents) | **Dva (paltaráh, tree, chitírye) rublyá (fúnta, dóllara, tsénta)** |
| | Два (полтора́, три, четы́ре) рубля́ (фу́нта, до́ллара, це́нта) |
| Two (1½, 3, 4) kopecks | **Dvyé (paltaríy, tree, chitírye) kapyéyky** |
| | Две (полторы́, три, четы́ре) копе́йки |
| Five (10, 100) roubles (pounds, dollars, cents, kopecks) | **Pyát (dyéssyit, stoh) rublyéy (fúntaf, dóllaraf, tséntaf, kapyéyik)** |
| | Пять (де́сять, сто) рубле́й (фу́нтов, до́лларов, це́нтов, копе́ек) |

*Ordinals*

| First | **Pyérvy (pyérvaya, pyérvaye, pyérviye)** | Пе́рвый (пе́рвая, пе́рвое, пе́рвые) |
| Second | **Ftaróy (ftaráya, ftaróye)** | Второ́й (втора́я, второ́е) |

| Third | **Tryéty (tryétya, tryétye)** | Тре́тий (тре́тья, тре́тые) |
|---|---|---|
| Fourth | **Chitvyórty (chitvyórtaya, chitvyórtaye)** | Четвёртый (четвёртая, четвёртое) |
| Fifth | **Pyáty (-aya, aye)** | Пя́тый (-ая, -ое) |
| Sixth | **Shistóy (-áya, -óye)** | Шесто́й (-а́я, -о́е) |
| Seventh | **Sidmóy (-áya, -óye)** | Седьмо́й (-а́я, -о́е) |
| Eighth | **Vasmóy (-áya, -óye)** | Восьмо́й (-а́я, -о́е) |
| Ninth | **Divyáty (-aya, -aye)** | Девя́тый (-ая, -ое) |
| Tenth | **Dissyáty (-aya, -aye)** | Деся́тый (-ая, -ое) |
| Eleventh | **Adéenatsaty (-aya, -aye)** | Оди́ннадцатый (-ая, -ое) |
| Twentieth | **Dvatsáty (-aya, -aye)** | Двадца́тый (-ая, -ое) |
| Twenty-fourth | **Dvátsat chitvyórty (-aya, -aye)** | Два́дцать чет-вёртый (-ая, -ое) |
| Thirtieth | **Tritsáty (-aya, -aye)** | Тридца́тый (-ая, -ое) |
| Fortieth | **Sarakavóy (-áya, -óye)** | Сороково́й (-а́я, -о́е) |
| Hundredth | **Sóty (-aya, -aye)** | Со́тый (-ая, -ое) |
| Thousandth | **Tíssyichny (-aya, -aye)** | Ты́сячный (-ая, -ое) |

| Today is May 21st | **Sivódnya dvátsat pyérvaye máya** Сего́дня два́дцать пе́рвое ма́я |
|---|---|
| We arrived on May 21st | **Mi priyezhály dvátsat pyérvaye máya** Мы прие́хали два́дцать пе́рвого ма́я |
| Room 5 is occupied; no. 6 is free | **Pyáty nómir zányit – shistóy svabódin** Пя́тый но́мер за́нят, – шесто́й свобо́ден |
| This room is on the second floor | **Éta kómnata na ftaróm etazhéh** Э́та ко́мната на второ́м этаже́ |

| | | |
|---|---|---|
| The Bank is the third building from the corner | **Bank – tryéty dom at ugláh** | Банк – тре́тый дом от угла́ |
| That street is the first turning on the right | **Éta úlitsa – pyérvy pavarót napráva** | Э́та у́лица – пе́рвый поворо́т напра́во |
| Our seats are in Row 10 | **Náshy mistáh v dissyátam ridú** | На́ши места́ в деся́том ряду́ |
| You will find this in chapter 20 of the book | **Vi naydyótye éta v dvatsátay glavyéh kneégy** | Вы найдёте э́то в двадца́той главе́ кни́ги |
| You will find this in paragraph 20 of the rules | **Vi naydyótye éta v dvatsátam parágrafye právil** | Вы найдёте э́то в двадца́том пара́графе пра́вил |
| The boy was born in 1956 | **Málchik radeélsya f tíssyicha divyitsót pitdissyát shistóm gadú** | Ма́льчик роди́тлся в ты́сяча девятьсо́т пятьдеся́т шесто́м году́ |
| The girl was born in 1953 | **Dyévachka radiláss f tíssyicha divyitsót pitdissyát tryétyim gadú** | Де́вочка родила́сь в ты́сяча девятьсо́т пятьдеся́т тре́тьем году́ |

# Money, measures, weights

| | | |
|---|---|---|
| Money | **Dyéngy** | Де́ньги |
| A coin | **Manyéta** | Моне́та |
| A bank note | **Bánkavsky bilyét** | Ба́нковский биле́т |
| Small change | **Myélach (myélkaya manyéta)** | Ме́лочь (ме́лкая моне́та) |
| A kopeck | **Kapyéyka** | Копе́йка |

| | | |
|---|---|---|
| A rouble | **rubl** | Рубль |
| Fifty kopecks | **Pitdissyát kapyéyik** | Пятьдеся́т копе́ек |
| Centimetre | **Santimyétr** | Сантиме́тр |
| Metre | **Myétr** | Метр |
| Kilometre | **Kilamyétr** | Киломе́тр |
| Square metre | **Kvadrátny myétr** | Квадра́тный метр |
| Cubic metre | **Kubéechisky myétr** | Куби́ческий метр |
| Hectare | **Giktár** | Гекта́р |
| Litre | **Léetr** | Литр |
| Hectolitre | **Giktaléetr** | Гектоли́тр |
| Gram | **Gramm** | Грамм |
| Kilogram (2½ lb) | **Kilagrámm** | Килогра́мм |
| Fifty kilograms | **Pitdissyát kilagrámaf** | Пятьдеся́ть кило-<br>гра́ммов |
| A hundred kilograms | **Stoh kilagrámmaf** | Сто килогра́ммов |
| A ton (1000 kilo-<br>grams) | **Tónna (tíssyicha<br>kilagrámmaf)** | То́нна (ты́сяча<br>килогра́ммов) |

| | |
|---|---|
| I have no change with me | **U minyá nyét s sabóy myélachy** |
| | У меня́ нет с собо́й ме́лочи |
| I only have a little silver | **U minyá tólka nimnóga siribráh** |
| | У меня́ то́лько немно́го<br>серебра́ |
| I only have large notes | **U minyá tólka krúpniye dyéngy** |
| | У меня́ то́лько кру́пные де́ньги |
| Can you change 100 roubles? | **Mózhitye vi razminyát stoh<br>rubléy?** |
| | Мо́жете вы разменя́ть сто<br>рубле́й? |
| I have lost a 50-rouble note | **Yá patiryál bumázhku (bilyét)<br>f pitdissyát rubléy** |
| | Я потеря́л бума́жку (биле́т)<br>в пятьдеся́т рубле́й |
| I must borrow £1 till tomorrow | **Yá dólzhin zanyát adéen funt do<br>záftra** |
| | Я до́лжен заня́ть оди́н фунт до<br>за́втра |

| | |
|---|---|
| Can you lend me 2 roubles and 50 kopecks | **Mózhitye vi adalzhéet mnyé dva rublyá pitdissyát kapyéyik?** |
| | Мо́жете вы одолжи́ть мне два рубля́ пятьдеся́т копе́ек? |
| Put a 10-kopeck piece in the slot | **Apustéetye manyétu v dyéssyit kapyéyik** |
| | Опусти́те моне́ту в де́сять копе́ек |
| How much do I owe you? | **Skólka yá vam dólzhin?** |
| | Ско́лько я вам до́лжен? |
| When will you be able to repay me? | **Kagdá vi smózhitye mnyé atdát?** |
| | Когда́ вы смо́жете мне отда́ть? |
| I have 2000 roubles to pay | **Yá dólzhin zaplatéet dvyé tíssyichy rubléy** |
| | Я до́лжен заплати́ть две ты́сячи рубле́й |
| I drove at a speed of fifty kilometres an hour | **Yá yékhal sa skórastyu f pitdissyát kilamyétraf f chass** |
| | Я е́хал со ско́ростью в пятьдеся́т киломе́тром в час |
| Let me have 3·40 metres of this ribbon | **Atryézhtye mnyé tree myétra sórak santimyétraf étay lyénty** |
| | Отре́жьте мне три ме́тра со́рок сантиме́тров э́той ле́нты |

## Countries and nationalities

| | *Place* | *Adjective* | *People* |
|---|---|---|---|
| Afghanistan | Афганиста́н | афга́нский | афга́нец |
| Africa | А́фрика | африка́нский | африка́нец |
| Albania | Алба́ния | алба́нский | алба́нец |
| America | Аме́рика | америка́нский | америка́нец |
| Arabia | Ара́вия | ара́бский | ара́б |
| Argentine | Аргенти́на | аргенти́нский | аргенти́нец |
| Asia | А́зия | азиа́тский | азиа́т |
| Australia | Австра́лия | австрали́йский | австрали́ец |
| Austria | А́встрия | австри́йский | австри́ец |

| | *Place* | *Adjective* | *People* |
|---|---|---|---|
| Belgium | Бе́льгия | бельги́йский | бельги́ец |
| Brazil | Брази́лия | брази́льский | брази́лец |
| Bulgaria | Болга́рия | болга́рский | болга́рин |
| Canada | Кана́да | кана́дский | кана́дец |
| Chile | Чи́ли | чили́йский | чили́ец |
| China | Кита́й | кита́йский | кита́ец |
| Czechoslovakia | Чехослова́кия | чехослова́цкий | чех |
| Denmark | Да́ния | да́тский | датча́нин |
| Egypt | Еги́пет | еги́петский | египтя́нин |
| England | А́нглия | англи́йский | англича́нин |
| Europe | Евро́па | европе́йский | европе́ец |
| Finland | Финля́ндия | фи́нский | финн |
| France | Фра́нция | францу́зский | францу́з |
| Germany | Герма́ния | неме́цкий | не́мец |
| Great Britain | Великобрита́ния | брита́нский | брита́нец |
| Greece | Гре́ция | гре́ческий | грек |
| Holland | Голла́ндия | голла́ндский | голла́ндец |
| Hungary | Ве́нгрия | венге́рский | венге́рец |
| Iceland | Исла́ндия | исла́ндский | исла́ндец |
| India | И́ндия | инду́сский | инду́с |
| Iraq | Ира́к | | |
| Israel | Изра́иль | изра́ильский | израели́т |
| Italy | Ита́лия | италья́нский | италья́нец |
| Japan | Япо́ния | япо́нский | япо́нец |
| Jugoslavia | Югосла́вия | югосла́вский | югосла́в |
| Manchuria | Манчжу́рия | манчжу́рский | манчжу́р |
| Mexico | Ме́ксика | мексика́нский | мексика́нкец |
| Mongolia | Монго́лия | монго́льский | монго́л |
| Norway | Норве́гия | норве́жский | норве́жец |
| Persia | Ира́н | ира́нский (перси́дский) | ира́нец (перс) |
| Poland | По́льша | по́льский | поля́к |
| Portugal | Португа́лия | португа́льский | португа́лец |
| Rumania | Румы́ния | румы́нский | румы́н |
| Spain | Испа́ния | испа́нский | испа́нец |
| Sweden | Шве́ция | шве́дский | швед |

|  | *Place* | *Adjective* | *People* |
|---|---|---|---|
| Switzerland | Швейца́рия | швейца́рский | швейца́рец |
| Turkey | Ту́рция | туре́цкий | ту́рок |
| United States | Соединённые Шта́ты Аме́рики (США) | | |
| USSR | СССР | сове́тский (ру́сский) | ру́сский |

## Abbreviations

The following information on Russian institutions may be useful:

### 1 *The Party*

| The Communist Party of the Whole Union | **Veh-Ka-Peh Vsyesayúznaya kamunistéechiskaya pártiya** |
|---|---|
| | ВКП (б): Всесою́зная комму-нисти́ческая па́ртия |
| The Central Committee of the Communist Party of the Whole Union | **Tseh-Ka-Veh-Ka-Peh Tsintrálny kamityét vsyesayúznay Kamunistéechiskay pártiy** |
| | ЦКВКП (б): Центра́льный комите́т всесою́зной комму-нисти́ческой па́ртии |
| Its Political Bureau | **Palitbyuroh: Palitéechiskaye byuróh** |
| | Политбюро́: Полити́ческое бюро́ |
| The Komsomol (= Young Communist League) | **Kamsamól: Kamunistéechisky sayúz maladyózhy** |
| | Комсомо́л: Коммунисти́-ческий сою́з молодёжи |

### 2 *The Government*

| The USSR (= Union of Soviet Socialist Republics) | **Ess-Ess-Ess-Err: Sayús Savyét-skikh Satsyalistéechiskikh Rispúblik** |
|---|---|
| | СССР: Сою́з Сове́тских Со-циалисти́ческих Респу́блик |

The RSFSR (=Russian Soviet Federal Socialist Republic)

**Err-Ess-Eff-Ess-Err: Rasséeskaya Savyétskaya Fidiratéevnaya Satsyalistéechiskaya Rispúblika**
РСФСР: Росси́йская Сове́тскауа Федерати́вная Социалисти́ческая Респу́блика

The Supreme Soviet (=Parliament): 2 'Houses':

**Vyerkhóvny Savyét**
Верхо́вный Сове́т

Soviet of Nationalities

**Savyét natsyonálnastyey**
Сове́т национа́льностей

Soviet of the Union

**Savyét Sayúza**
Сове́т Сою́за

(Soviet = Council)

KGB (=Ministry of the Interior)

**Ka-Geh-Beh: Kamityét Gassudárstvinnay Bisapássnasty**
КГБ: Комите́т госуда́рственной безопа́сности

Minindel (=Ministry of Foreign Affairs)

**Minindyél: Ministyérstva inastránnikh dyél**
Мининде́л: Министе́рство иностра́нных дел

## 3 *Learned bodies*

Ak. n. (=Academy of Science)

**Ak En: Akadyémya Naúk**
Ак. н.: Акаде́мия нау́к

VUZ (=Institution of higher education)

**Vuz: Vísheye uchébnaye zavidyénye**
ВУЗ: Вы́сшее уче́бное заведе́ние

VOKS (=Society for Cultural Relations with foreign countries)

**Vsyesayúznaye óbshistva kultúrnay svyázy z zagranéetsey**
Всесою́зное о́бщество культу́рной свя́зи с заграни́цей

## 4 *Miscellaneous*

| | |
|---|---|
| State Bank | **Gossbánk: Gassudárstvinny bank** |
| | Госба́нк: Госуда́рственный банк |
| State Planning authority | **Gossplan: Gossudárstvinny plan (gossudárstvinnaya plánavaya kaméessiya)** |
| | Госпла́н: Госуда́рственный план (госуда́рственная пла́новая коми́ссия) |
| Five-Year Plan | **Pitilyétka – Pitilyétny plan** |
| | Пятиле́тка: Пятиле́тный план |
| Collective farm | **Kalkhós – Kallikteévnaye khazyáystva** |
| | Колхо́з: коллекти́вное хозя́йство |
| State farm | **Savkhós – Savyétskaye khazyáystva** |
| | Совхо́з: сове́тское хозя́йство |
| State Department Store in Moscow | **Gum – Gassudárstvinny univirsálny magazéen** |
| | ГУМ: Госуда́рственный универса́льный магази́н |

## 5 *Signs used in this book*

| | |
|---|---|
| Et cetera | и др. = и други́е |
| And so on | и т. д. = и так да́лее |
| And such like | и т. п. = и тому́ подо́бное |
| And so forth | и пр. = и про́чее |
| For example | напр. = наприме́р |

**ARABIC PHRASE BOOK**
**FRENCH PHRASE BOOK**
**GERMAN PHRASE BOOK**
**GREEK PHRASE BOOK**
**ITALIAN PHRASE BOOK**
**SERBO CROAT PHRASE BOOK**
**SPANISH PHRASE BOOK**

These phrase books, in a handy pocket size, will help you to be readily understood on all everyday occasions; to get you quickly and easily, where you want and what you want; and to enable you to cope with those minor problems and emergencies that always seem to arise on holiday. A pronunciation guide accompanies each phrase, the topic of which can quickly be found by reference to the contents list or index. Subjects include: customs, medical treatment, shopping, sightseeing, restaurants, cafés and bars.

**TEACH YOURSELF BOOKS**